Studies in the History of Art
Published by the National Gallery of Art,
Washington

This series includes: Studies in the History of
Art, collected papers on objects in the Gallery's
collections and other art-historical studies (formerly *Report and Studies in the History of
Art*); Monograph Series I, a catalogue of stained
glass in the United States; Monograph Series II,
on conservation topics; and Symposium Papers
(formerly Symposium Series), the proceedings
of symposia sponsored by the Center for
Advanced Study in the Visual Arts at the
National Gallery of Art.

---

* Forthcoming

Conservation Research: Studies of
Fifteenth- to Nineteenth-Century Tapestry

Conservation Research

Studies of Fifteenth- to Nineteenth-Century Tapestry

Edited by Lotus Stack

National Gallery of Art, Washington

Distributed by the University Press of New England

Hanover and London

This publication was produced by the Editors Office, National Gallery of Art, Washington
Editor-in-Chief, Frances P. Smyth
Printed by Collins Lithographing, Inc., Baltimore, Maryland

The text paper is 80 pound LOE Dull text with matching cover
The type is Trump Medieval, set by Artech Graphics II, Inc., Baltimore, Maryland

The symposium was made possible by
The Circle of the National Gallery of Art

Distributed by the University Press of New England, 23 South Main Street, Hanover, New Hampshire 03755

Abstracted by RILA (International Repertory of the Literature of Art), Williamstown, Massachusetts 01267

Selected papers presented October 9–10, 1989, at a symposium held in memory of Joseph V. Columbus by the Division of Conservation, National Gallery of Art

ISSN 0091–7338
ISBN 0–89468–183–4

Cover: The Mazarin Tapestry (detail), c. 1500, Netherlandish. National Gallery of Art, Washington, Widener Collection, 1942.9.446

Note to the Reader: Dimensions of works of art in figure captions are given height before width, first in centimeters, then in inches.

Contents

Foreword

The National Gallery of Art has had the pleasure of organizing a tapestry symposium in honor of the late Joseph V. Columbus, who joined the Gallery in 1969 and worked to preserve its fine tapestry collection until his retirement in 1989. During his thirty-five years of professional dedication to the care of textiles, his innovations in the care of tapestries gained him an important place in an international field. He lectured throughout the United States and abroad on textiles and their history, contributing to the education of students in training programs and participating in professional meetings that encompassed an extensive range of topics related to the care and preservation of textiles. The choice of the image on the cover of this volume is a sentimental one; the *Mazarin Tapestry* was Joe Columbus' favorite.

Tapestries historically have been associated with persons of wealth and power and thus have played an important role in the world's artistic heritage. Unlike other areas of art, however, relatively little is known or understood about the sources, subjects, and creation of some of these magnificent works. A tapestry symposium provides a valuable opportunity to cast new light on these questions and bring renewed recognition of the importance of these sumptuous objects in the traditions and history of art in the Western world.

The papers included in this volume were among those presented at the symposium by a distinguished group of participants representing diverse professional as well as geographical backgrounds. The individual concerns expressed, covering a variety of subjects of art historical significance, technical importance, and issues regarding conservation, demonstrate the broad range of research in the field of textiles.

The publication of these papers by the National Gallery as a volume in Monograph Series II, a series within *Studies in the History of Art* devoted to conservation issues, is evidence of the importance of conservation in the management of our collections. We are indebted to the support given the symposium and this publication by The Circle of the National Gallery of Art. The sharing of this information is also a fitting tribute to Joseph Columbus' memory.

EARL A. POWELL III
Director

Introduction

The papers presented in this volume were delivered at a symposium convened to honor Joseph V. Columbus, the National Gallery's textile conservator from 1969 to 1989. Therefore it is natural that the foremost tapestry scholars of the day were invited to participate in this event. Conservation specialists as well as art historians were involved in this celebration. This mix was fitting, for Mr. Columbus was one of the first textile conservators to realize the importance of combining safety of the object with an aesthetic presentation of textiles. He fully understood that textiles were distinctive and should not be forced into rigid presentations that denied their intrinsic qualities; too often in the past textiles had been presented to the public in a formal manner related to painting installations, as if to remind the audience that these objects too were "art."

In the 1950s and 1960s, while Joseph Columbus was the conservator at the Textile Museum in Washington, he and his colleague James Rice initiated a series of classes to train textile conservation specialists. Prior to this time there was no specific training in the United States for professionals in this area. The combined expertise of the two men created a program that influenced the professional standards in the field for decades. Rice stressed a disciplined scientific understanding of textile materials and environment. Building on Rice's scientific approach, Columbus was able to enhance the visual impact of presentation yet emphasize the importance of preservation of the object, a combination that made the Textile Museum program unique. The students who received this training became specialized conservators in the country's major museums with important textile holdings, and in turn their students have continued to maintain that balance of physical responsibility for and artistic responsiveness to individual textile presentations.

Later in his career, working free-lance and in museums, Columbus experimented with a number of techniques, and over the years he developed specific procedures that continue to be used with success. His work established a basic approach to textile conservation that set criteria for cleaning, gave attention to structural alignment, and developed supportive mounting systems and storage formats, establishing principles that are standard in conservation today. However, he made his major contribution in the philosophical areas of understanding the need to unite presentation with preservation.

LOTUS STACK
Editor

Acknowledgments

The organization of this symposium would not have been possible without the enthusiasm of the National Gallery's director emeritus, J. Carter Brown, for conservation programs and the publication of related material for the museum community. Likewise, our gratitude goes to Earl A. Powell III, director of the Gallery, and to John Wilmerding, past deputy director of the Gallery, and his successor, Roger Mandle, for bringing this symposium and publication to fruition. The efforts of Mary Ashton, former head of the Gallery's textile conservation department, and those of her assistant, Julia Burke, were substantial. Lotus Stack of the Minneapolis Institute of Arts offered insight and valued suggestions for the manuscripts. Special thanks must be extended to Frances Smyth, the Gallery's editor-in-chief, and Jane Sweeney, editor; our gratitude goes also to Janice Gruver, editorial coordinator, and Michael Skalka, program coordinator, in the conservation division.

The generosity of the Circle of the National Gallery of Art made the Joseph V. Columbus Tapestry Symposium and this volume possible. We are indebted to the speakers at the symposium and the authors of the essays who willingly shared their knowledge. And most of all we thank Joe Columbus, who brought textile conservation and presentation to new standards and recognition.

ROSS M. MERRILL
Chief of Conservation

EDITH A. STANDEN

Madame de Pompadour's Gobelins Tapestries

Although the marquise de Pompadour was a greater patron of the Sèvres porcelain works than she was of the Gobelins tapestry manufactory, tapestries were nonetheless part of the decoration of her many residences. During her nearly twenty years in a prominent position at the court of Louis xv, she acquired a substantial number of tapestries. The Gobelins manufactory, which had been set up nearly a century earlier to supply furnishings for the royal palaces, still worked primarily for the king, but Madame de Pompadour did not usually receive its tapestries as outright gifts; for the most part, she bought, borrowed, and exchanged them as a private individual. As a result, the archives of the manufactory, so comprehensive and precise where the king's belongings and money were concerned, contain very little information about her tapestries.[1] Which of them adorned her rooms must in most cases be deduced from the incidental letter, memorandum, or bill that has survived, supplemented by the inventory and sales catalogues of her possessions made after her death on 15 April 1764.[2] Her brother's sales catalogues are also sources of information.[3]

The earliest document mentioning a Gobelins tapestry connected with Madame de Pompadour is dated 27 December 1751; it is a memorandum listing the expenses incurred by Pierre François Cozette, head of a workshop at the Gobelins, when he took to Versailles "le tableau de tapisserie de haute lisse, d'après l'original d'Ostade, presenté au Roy par M. le Directeur général."[4] The *directeur général des bâtiments* at the time was the newly appointed Abel Poisson de Vandières, later the marquis de Marigny, Madame de Pompadour's brother. The bill included the cost of a frame and glass cover for the tapestry (indicating that the piece was small), the wages of two men to carry it, and "le transport de Bellevëue à Versailles." Madame de Pompadour had acquired the chateau of Bellevue in 1749, and evidently the tapestry had been there before her brother ordered it to be given to the king.

Strangely enough, Madame de Pompadour appears to have owned a similar Gobelins picture at her death. Her inventory includes an item described as

Une femme tenant un enfant et appuyée sur sa porte; ce morceau est fait en petits points par NEILSON *aux Gobelins, d'après* Adrien van Ostade, *sous glace et bordure dorée.*[5]

This description is nonsense; "petit point" is embroidery on canvas, a technique used mainly by amateurs that certainly would not have been employed by the men in the Gobelins workshop headed by Jacques Neilson. He is not known to have produced small tapestry pictures, which were apparently something of a specialty of Cozette's.

A further complication is introduced by the appearance of a more fully described small tapestry in the 1782 sale catalogue of works of art owned by Marigny. Under the heading "Ostade (Adrien van)" is the entry:

Un sujet supérieurement rendu, en tapisserie, par le sieur Cozette, à la Manufacture royale des Gobelins, représentant une femme hollandaise tenant son enfant dans ses bras et appuyée sur le bas de la porte de sa maison. Le tableau capital de ce maître a fait partie du célèbre cabinet qu'avait M. le Duc de Choiseul. Ce morceau est sous glace de 39 pouces sur 30 de longueur. [The *pied* and the *pouce* were almost the same as the foot and the inch.][6]

The mention of the duc de Choiseul enables us to know the appearance of this tapestry, as engravings of his collection were published in 1771 (fig. 1).[7] Marigny may well have inherited the tapestry from his sister; one of his sales catalogues includes the statement "la plus grande partie des objets contenus du présent catalogue provient de la succession de madame la marquise de Pompadour."[8]

These confusing documents are difficult to interpret. We are apparently dealing with a single composition, but how many times was it woven at the Gobelins and by which workshops? Were there three similar tapestries owned by the king, by his most famous mistress, and by her brother? As this seems unlikely, the simplest answer would be that there was a single tapestry, presented to the king in 1751, returned to Madame de Pompadour, and inherited by her brother. She had other small tapestries. Marigny owned a François Boucher painting of *Venus Asking Vulcan for Arms for Aeneas*, a subject frequently painted by this artist; it was sixteen *pouces* square and was described in the sale catalogue as "exécutée en tapisserie pour madame de Pompadour."[9] Madame de Pompadour's inventory included a framed picture of Saint Anne, found in a cupboard, "de petits points des Gobelins," again, most probably, a small woven tapestry.[10] The compiler of the inventory, in his haste, may have been deceived by the extreme fineness of the

1. Unknown engraver after Adriaen van Ostade, *Woman and Child in Doorway*, 1771, engraving on paper, 15 x 12 (6 x 4¾)
Thomas J. Watson Library, The Metropolitan Museum of Art, New York

2. Weavers of the Gobelins Manufactory after Claude Audran the Younger, *Neptune*, 1736, wool and silk tapestry, 354 x 174 (138 x 65)
Collection du Mobilier National, Paris

3. François Boucher, *The Rising of the Sun*, 1753, oil on canvas, 321 x 270 (126½ x 106½) The Wallace Collection, London

4. François Boucher, *The Setting of the Sun*, 1753, oil on canvas, 324 x 264 (127½ x 104) The Wallace Collection, London

weaving; comparable small eighteenth-century tapestries have as many as ten warps to the centimeter.

Madame de Pompadour made more important acquisitions of tapestries in 1751. She probably ordered her first set of tapestry upholstery (this will be considered later, with her other commissions for furniture covers). Her brother directed the storeroom of the Gobelins to send four *Portières des dieux* to Bellevue;[11] these may have been a loan, or possibly the marquise did not keep them, as there is no further record of them. Well over a hundred pieces from this series of narrow tapestries, with or without gold thread and with several different borders, had been woven by 1751, and there is no way of telling which deities Madame de Pompadour placed in front of her doors at Bellevue as there were eight possible choices (fig. 2). The designs of the series had been ordered from Claude Audran the Younger as early as 1699 and, though thoroughly up to date when painted, they

would not have seemed modern half a century later.

On 4 January 1752, however, Madame de Pompadour was mentioned in connection with new designs in a letter by Cozette:

Madame la Marquise ayant eu la bonté de jetter les yeux sur moy pour luy exécuter deux pièces d'après M. Boucher destinées pour Bellevëue, dont le premier tableau doit estre fait à la fin de ce mois.[12]

These tapestries were after two of Boucher's most radiant paintings, depictions of Apollo called *The Rising of the Sun* and *The Setting of the Sun*, now in the Wallace Collection, London (figs. 3 and 4).[13] They show the god of the sun, representing Louis XV, reluctantly leaving his beloved Thetis at dawn and leaping from his chariot to embrace her at close of day. Madame de Pompadour owned these paintings until her death.[14] They are more than ten feet high, and the tapestries after them must have been as splendid as any ever made at the Gobelins. Boucher, thoroughly familiar with tapestry design after a decade of work for the Beauvais manufactory, was at the height of his powers, and the weavers undoubtedly did their utmost to please the royal mistress.

When, with Madame de Pompadour's permission, the paintings were to be shown at the Salon of 1753, Cozette was ordered to relinquish them temporarily to Boucher, who put the date 1753 on them. The tapestries are listed in the official manufactory records with the usual details: dimensions, date of weaving, workshop, and cost—in this case the substantial sum of nearly 5,000 *livres*. These are the statistics recorded for all Gobelins tapestries woven for the king, but Cozette again mentioned one of the pair in a letter to Vandières as "la pièce d'après M. Boucher, que j'ay l'honneur d'exécuter en tapisserie pour Madame Votre Soeur."[15] They must have been direct gifts from the king. He is not, however, recorded as having paid for the paintings, as he would have done if they were to be kept at the manufactory. Madame de Pompadour must have bought them herself and kept them, thereby ensuring that no more tapestries after these designs were woven.

The *Apollo* tapestries were finished by 1754 and hung at Bellevue. It was somewhat unusual to commission only two; a set of four or six pieces, to cover all the walls of a room, was more common. Perhaps the two *Apollos* were hung in an alcove on either side of a state bed, as tapestries sometimes were at this date.[16] This arrangement would certainly have been appropriate at Bellevue. The chateau was sold to the king in 1757, when Madame de Pompadour evidently planned to move the tapestries to her house in Paris, the Hôtel d'Evreux or Hôtel de Pompadour (now known as the Palais de l'Elysée); but she found them of insufficient height for the designated space. Several letters have survived that tell what happened. Her brother wrote to the man then in charge of the royal manufactories, the great architect Jean Germain Sufflot, on 12 September 1757:

Vous connaissez, monsieur, les deux pièces de tapisserie que ma soeur a fait exécuter aux Gobelins d'après les dessins de M. Boucher. Elles étaient justes pour la place qu'elles occu-paient à Bellevue. Il est aujourd'hui nécessaire de les augmenter d'une bordure pour la nouvelle place qui leur est destinée. Ma soeur desire que le dessin de ces bordures soit fait par M. Boucher et qu'elles soient relatives au sujet des tapisseries; arrangez-vous sur ce avec MM. Boucher et Cozette, et faites-moi une réponse par écrit que je communiquerai à ma soeur.[17]

Soufflot wasted no time and was able to answer a week later:

Monsieur, j'ai été ces jours derniers à l'Hôtel de Pompadour pour y vérifier les mesures que m'avoit remises M. le Queustre [Madame de Pompadour's upholsterer]; en examinant la place où doivent être mises les deux pièces de tapisserie faites d'après les tableaux de M. Boucher, j'ai vu que les bordures dont elles ont besoin pour la remplir auraient dix-huit à dix-neuf pouces de largeur; j'avais ensuite pris parole de M. Boucher pour aller aujourd'hui aux Gobelins y examiner les différentes bordures de la manufacture; nous y avons passé la matinée, et y sommes convenus de la forme de celles que vous m'ordonnez; comme c'est affaire d'ornement et que le sieur Jacques [Maurice Jacques, a flower painter at the Gobelins] le peint fort bien, M. Boucher lui a donné ses idées, et moi les mesures, pour qu'il en fasse une esquisse, d'après laquelle il fera les tableaux pour l'exécution; pendant ce tems-là on préparera les toiles afin que Mme la Marquise puisse être satisfaite promptement; pour peindre ces bordures plus dans le vrai nous avons pensé qu'il serait bon de s'aider de la nature, et comme il y en a, Mon-sieur, de fort belles en bois doré au magasin du Luxembourg qui sont demontées, j'ai passé chez M. Bailly; [garde général of the king's paintings] pour le prier d'en délivrer quelques parties, qu'on lui rendra ensuite, à MM. Belle [Clement Belle, a Gobelins artist] et Boucher qui ont du les choisir cet après-midi; celles que l'on fera d'après imiteront mieux la dorure, et elles seront enrichies d'attributs d'Apollon, des fleurs et des fruits qu'il fait croîtres, et des branches de corail et autres productions de la mer que l'on voit dans les deux sujets.[18]

Marigny approved the project and visited the manufactory while the borders were being woven. We learn this from a letter that Soufflot wrote to him on 2 October 1758, asking to have the designs paid for by the king:

Vous avez vû à la Manufacture Royale des Gobelins, sur les metiers, les bordures qui s'y

*exécutent pour Madame La Marquise de Pom-
padour, elle en a fait payer les traits pris sur
les tableaux par M. Boizot* [Antoine Boizot, a
Gobelins artist], *et qui estoient nécessaires à
M. Cozette pour l'éxecution; comme ces
tableaux sont considérables et riches de fleurs
et d'ornements faits avec beaucoup de soin,
ils pourront servir longtems pour les ouvrages
du Roy, et pour cette raison je pense, Monsieur,
qu'ils seront payés par les* Bâtiments [i.e., by the
royal treasury]; *ils ont occupés longtems Mr.
Jacques qui a suivi avec zèle les conseils de Mr.
Boucher et fait avec plaisir les changements
qu'il a pu désirer dans le cour de l'ouvrage.*[19]

Soufflot quoted a price of 2,000 *livres* for
the cartoon, but there is no record that it
was actually paid by the king rather than
by Madame de Pompadour, and no later
use of the border design is known. A cartoon in the Mobilier National for a tapestry border by Jacques, showing Apollo's
lyre and a sunburst with a multitude of
flowers, has been considered the one used
for the *Apollo* tapestries.[20]

One must remember that Boucher and
Soufflot were highly successful and extremely busy professionals who could
hardly have wished to spend their time
examining and measuring borders and
frames. Boucher in particular must have
had cause for anxiety; he had been told to
design the borders himself but had merely
contributed ideas and criticism. Madame
de Pompadour expected to be obeyed.

A few years later, Madame de Pompadour made what today seems an incom-
prehensible decision to exchange the
Apollo tapestries for sets of the series
known as the *Enfants jardiniers* and the
Métamorphoses. Perhaps the *Apollo* pair
reminded her only too poignantly that her
Apollo, while still finding her company
indispensable, was no longer eager to
share her bed. The tapestries went back to
the manufactory; their value was then estimated to be over 4,000 *livres* each, an increase due presumably to the new borders.
They were later offered for sale several
times, and were then described as having
been hung for a number of years at Bellevue without borders, so that the latter
were now "plus fraiches que les pièces."[21]
Finally they were sold in 1768 for a good
deal less than their original cost. Neilson,
who arranged the transaction, justified the

low price by saying they were ten years
old and "ont beaucoup perdu de leur
fraicheur."[22] They are not now known to
exist. Because Neilson sold so many Gobelins tapestries, old and new, to Englishmen,
it has been suggested that Madame de
Pompadour's pair were among them, but
there is no documentation of such a sale.

Two other tapestries that were probably
used in Madame de Pompadour's Paris
hôtel were sent back to the manufactory
in 1758, but they had been loans. Their arrival in Madame de Pompadour's collection
is recorded in a letter from her brother to
the then-director of the Gobelins, Garnier
d'Isle, dated 6 October 1753. Marigny
asked him to tell the man in charge of the
Gobelins storeroom to send an *April* and
an *October* from the series *Douze mois de
l'année* (usually known as the *Months of
Lucas*) to Madame de Pompadour as a loan
from the king. They are recorded as out of
the manufactory from 1754 to 1758.[23]
These large pieces, almost ten feet square,
were woven in 1733–1734 (*April*) and 1743
(*October*) respectively, and probably had
borders with royal insignia designed in
1730. The central subjects, however, are
derived from a set of sixteenth-century
Brussels tapestries in the king's collection. Several pieces have survived of the
set from which Madame de Pompadour's
tapestries were taken, but not her pair;
their appearance is known from examples
of these months in other sets, although
these have different borders (fig. 5). The
activities depicted—boating, making
music, and a convivial open-air party—
would have seemed suitable for one of
Madame de Pompadour's country houses,
but the tapestries were apparently hung in
Paris. The duc de Luynes wrote in his
memoirs on 2 September 1754 that he had
seen the "nouvelle maison de Mme de
Pompadour" and added:

*Il y a actuellement dans le grand salon une
tapisserie faite aux Gobelins encadrée dans la
menuiserie. Dans le milieu de ces pièces de
tapisseries il y a deux L. L. surmontées d'une
courone.*[24]

The two *L*s for Louis indicate that these
tapestries were made for the king. The
duke was clearly shocked.

In her later acquisitions of tapestries, Madame de Pompadour seems to have wanted quantity, since, as has been mentioned, she exchanged the two *Apollo* tapestries for sets of what must have seemed by then old-fashioned designs. The *Enfant jardiniers* series began as outdoor scenes with winged children (actually *Amours jardiniers*). They were narrow panels (*entrefenêtres*) accompanying a series of the *Seasons* after Charles Le Brun, first woven before 1673. The children were later shown without wings, and Le Brun's designs were altered by a number of artists to make four large hangings representing the seasons; two scenes of children at work in a garden (an additional *Spring*) and a vineyard (an additional *Autumn*) were added to constitute a series of six pieces.[25]

The seventh weaving of the designs, which included five pieces from the series (the four original *Seasons* and the second *Spring*), was put on the looms in 1717 and finished in 1720. This set, with another *Summer* from an earlier weaving, hung from 1750 in the office of Le Normant de Tournehem (the lover of Madame de Pompadour's mother and the uncle of her husband) when he was *directeur général des bâtiments*. In 1752, after his death, these tapestries went back to the Gobelins storeroom and remained there until Soufflot was ordered to deliver them to Madame de Pompadour. The documents concerning the exchange of the two *Apollo* tapestries for this set date from 1760 to 1761. Madame de Pompadour acquired the chateau of Menars in 1760, and the tapestries were there at her death, when her brother inherited them. No record of them after 1777 has been located,[26] but they must have resembled the set made for the princesse de Conti, who died in 1739 (fig. 6).

Also in Le Normant de Tournehem's offices were three tapestries from the *Métamorphoses* series, sent there in 1747, at which time they were described as "fort anciennes" (very old). They were among seven pieces that had indeed been woven as early as 1714–1720, the only set of this complicated series to be recorded in full in the Gobelins archives. They were re-

5. Workshop of Michel Audran at the Gobelins Manufactory after an unknown Flemish sixteenth-century designer, *April*, 1732–1737, wool and silk tapestry, 361 x 269 (132 x 106)
The Metropolitan Museum of Art, New York, Gift of John D. Rockefeller, Jr., 1944

turned to the storeroom in 1755. The king gave permission to Madame de Pompadour to purchase these tapestries, and on 20 December 1760 Marigny instructed Soufflot to send her the complete set. Her payment of nearly 9,000 *livres* was made on 11 June 1761 after the tapestries had been altered and repaired.[27]

The *Métamorphoses* tapestries illustrate stories from Ovid, with the exception of one representation of Rinaldo and Armida, and were designed by Louis de Boulogne, Nicolas Bertin, Antoine Dieu,

6. Weavers of the Gobelins Manufactory after Charles Le Brun and François Desportes, *Spring*, before 1739, wool and silk tapestry, 355 x 225 (138 x 86) Collection du Mobilier National, Paris

Charles de La Fosse, and Antoine Coypel, working in a style decidedly old-fashioned by 1760.[28] Madame de Pompadour's set is not mentioned by this name (the *Métamorphoses*) in any later document, but possibly it was the "Quatre pièces de tapisserie des Gobelins, représentant les *Amours des dieux*" in a bedroom at

Menars and other *Amours des dieux* in another bedroom.[29] The compositions are known from the many other weavings of the series, all made for private customers (fig. 7).

Marigny, however, had an up-to-date *Amours des dieux* set, made up of four scenes after Boucher, Carle Van Loo, Jean Baptiste Pierre, and Joseph Marie Vien; the ten-foot-high paintings were shown in the 1757 Salon.[30] The following year each artist also painted *Tableaux d'enfants* (paintings of children), of the same height but narrow (about three to five feet), for tapestries called *trumeaux* (piers, narrow uprights) in Marigny's set; Pierre and Vien made two each, Van Loo and Boucher one each. Weaving of the first set was not completed until 1759. During that year four paintings of children, "le tout sur leur chassis" (all on their mounts), with the cartoon for the borders of the *Apollo* tapestries and "plusieurs tableaux de meubles" (several paintings for furniture), were taken from the Gobelins to the Hôtel de Pompadour and back again, at a cost of twenty-four *livres* including tips, charged to the king, as such errands often were.

Madame de Pompadour, having evidently seen and liked these paintings, wanted them and others like them as tapestries; Belle submitted a bill in 1760 for enlarging a painting by Van Loo "pour le mettre à la grandeur nécessaire pour la pièce commandée par Mme la Marquise de Pompadour"[31] and for taking Vien's painting back to his studio in the Louvre for additions. There is also a record of canvas supplied to enlarge Boucher's painting the same year and a bill dated 1761 for cleaning and varnishing a *Génies des sciences* by Noël Hallé and a *Génies des arts* by Boucher. These paintings had been made that year; Hallé's was in the 1761 Salon, the catalogue noting that it was "destineé à exécuter en tapisserie dans la Manufacture des Gobelins." Both are about ten feet square and are now in the Musée des Beaux-Arts, Angers (figs. 8 and 9).

Madame de Pompadour's set of the *Tableaux d'enfants* that were considered part of the *Amours des dieux* was woven as a private commission and consequently does not appear in the records of the man-

7. Weavers of the Gobelins Manufactory after Nicolas Bertin, *Apollo and the Serpent Python*, 1700–1730, wool and silk tapestry, 333 x 400 (130 x 151)
The Cleveland Museum of Art, Gift of Mrs. Matthias Plum

8. François Boucher, *Les Génies des arts*, 1761, oil on canvas, 320 x 320 (125 x 125)
Musée des Beaux-Arts, Angers

9. Noël Hallé, *Les Génies de la poèsie, de l'histoire, de la physique, et de l'astronomie*, 1761, oil on canvas, 320 x 320 (125 x 125)
Musée des Beaux-Arts, Angers

10. Workshop of Jacques Neilson at the Gobelins manufactory after François Boucher, *Les Génies des arts*, 1761–1764, wool and silk tapestry
Mr. and Mrs. J. C. Griffin, Grosse Pointe Farms, Michigan

11. Workshop of Pierre François Cozette at the Gobelins manufactory after Jean Baptiste Pierre, *Amours jouant avec des fleurs*, 1761, wool and silk tapestry, 313 x 261 (123 x 102)
Sold by Couturiez-Nicolay, Hôtel Drouot, Paris, 23 March 1982, no. 124

ufactory. Its existence is known from Belle's bill mentioned above and from the inventory of the Hôtel de Pompadour made after her death. This includes an entry concerning the Gobelins tapestry brought to her Paris *hôtel* by Audran and Cozette on 20 August 1764:

Douze aunes trois seizes un quart [the *aune* was divided into sixteen *bâtons*] *de tapisserie basse lisse, fabrique des Gobelins, representant les* Génies des Arts *et Sujets des* Amours des Dieux.[32]

It is unlikely, however, that Madame de Pompadour ever saw these tapestries. They were not brought to her house until August, and she had died in April. Her brother had tried to stop this delivery in a private letter of 20 June to the man in charge:

Il faudrait, Soufflot, tâcher de placer à quelque Anglais ou autrement les tapisseries que ma soeur avait ordonnées aux Gobelins et qu'elle avait payées. Je vous demande sur cela tout le zèle et l'activité que vous mettez aux choses qui m'intéressent.[33]

The end of the Seven Years War in 1763 had brought many English customers to the Gobelins, but Marigny's appeal was unsuccessful.

The set Madame de Pompadour ordered and paid for is known to have included Hallé's *Génies des sciences*, or, as it was called in the Salon, *Les Génies de la poésie, de l'histoire, de la physique, et de l'astronomie*. The design is not known to have been woven again, and the original tapestry has not been located. A tapestry after Boucher's painting, the *Génies des arts* (fig. 10) was also probably woven only once.[34] A tapestry sold at the Hôtel Drouot, Paris, 23 March 1982 (fig. 11) is taken from Pierre's painting of *Enfants* formerly in the palace of Fontainebleau;[35] it has Cozette's name and the date 1761. Since Marigny's tapestry of this design was made in 1759 and none of the *Enfants* was woven again, this piece is presumably the one owned by Madame de Pompadour. The records quoted above show that she must also have ordered Boucher's, Vien's, and Van Loo's *Enfants*, now known only

12. François Boucher, *La Cible d'amour*, 1758, oil on canvas, 268 x 167 (107 x 68) Musée du Louvre, Paris. ©R.M.N.

13. Joseph Marie Vien, *Enfants avec deux cygnes*, 1758, oil on canvas, 260 x 164 (106 x 67) Palais de Fontainebleau

from paintings in the Louvre and at Fontainebleau (figs. 12, 13, 14, and 15). Of these, the narrow panel (fig. 14) is presumably for one of Marigny's *trumeaux*.

When some tapestry cartoons were taken to the Hôtel de Pompadour in 1759, as has been described, "plusieurs tableaux des meubles" were among them. These were presumably cartoons for the tapestries that Soufflot spoke of in a letter to Marigny of 10 September 1757:

J'ai demandé à M. Neilson un fond d'un blanc bleuâtre qui, je le crois, fera briller les fleurs [Jacques' specialty] et s'accordéra avec la boiserie de la chambre dont le fonds sera blanc verni et les moulures dorées ainsi que les bois des fauteuils.[36]

Jacques later submitted a bill for designs for the backs, seats, and armrests of five armchairs and a sofa, described as:

Dix tableaux composés et varié de différents jets de fleurs coloriés avec bordures d'ornemens, entrelassées de petites fleurs, et plus dix tableaux (petits) pours les manchettes. . . . Deux tableaux l'un de 6 p.½, l'autre de 7 p.½, ornés de fleurs et d'une bordure d'ornemens composées et analogues aux dits tableaux cy-dessus, et deux petits tableaux pour les manchettes.[37]

A five-screen design was added in 1759, and two more designs for an armchair in 1760. Marigny's furniture, when delivered the following year, consisted of a screen, a sofa, and twelve armchairs, each chair back and seat design apparently used twice.

Madame de Pompadour evidently liked the upholstery cartoons brought to her house in 1759 as much as she did the *Enfants*, but every chair for her set had to be different and she needed two sofas. Jacques was accordingly put to work again and submitted a bill in 1760:

*Vingt dessins pour fauteuils, tant fonds que
dossiers, peint et coloriés à la gouache, for-
mant différents groupes de fleurs dans les
milieux refermés d'une petite bordure de
fleurs pour déterminer le listel.*[38]

Designs for a tall six-leaf screen were
included. The cost of the cartoons was
charged to the king, as they would remain
in the manufactory and be available for
other sets. What had already been woven
after these designs must have been among
the pieces brought to the Hôtel de Pompadour in August 1764, as the inventory of
this house includes "Le dessus de dix fauteuils complets en fleurs et ornements fond
blanc et mordoré. . . . Le dessus de deux
canapés de 7 pieds 6 p. de long sur 3 pieds
6 p. de profondeur, un sans dossier. . . .

Un paravent de six feuilles de pareil
tapisserie des Gobelins. . . . Un petit
écran."[39] The tapestries were apparently
unmounted.

There is a substantial amount of
Gobelins tapestry upholstery with designs
of flowers by Maurice Jacques and another
Gobelins artist, Louis Tessier, but by far
the largest number of pieces have red
grounds.[40] White grounds, Marigny's
"blanc bleuâtre" (bluish white), presumably the "fond paille" (straw ground) of
the "meubles des Gobelins" in his
chateau of Roule,[41] or Madame de
Pompadour's white and red, "fond blanc
et mordoré," are comparatively rare, but a
set of furniture in the National Gallery of
Art, Washington (ten armchairs, two
sofas, and a panel like the back of one of

16. Armchair, French or British nineteenth-century, and Gobelins tapestry
National Gallery of Art, Washington, 1942.9.434, Widener Collection

17. Maurice Jacques, *Modèle pour fond de fauteuil*, c. 1750, gouache on paper, 78 x 73 (30½ x 28½)
Collection du Mobilier National, Paris

the chairs, mounted as a firescreen) has tapestry upholstery corresponding exactly to Jacques' description of flowers and ornamental borders interlaced with small flowers (fig. 16). The *modèles* (cartoons) for the sofa, two chair-backs, and two chair-seats are in the Mobilier National (fig. 17). Two detached panels in the Metropolitan Museum of Art repeat the designs of two chair-backs in the National Gallery of Art set.[42] A set of furniture in the Madame d'Yvon sale, Galerie Georges Petit, Paris, 30 May–4 June 1892, no. 663 (ten armchairs and a sofa) and an armchair in the Musée des arts décoratifs, Paris, have similar upholstery. There are several firescreen panels with red or white grounds, some of them inscribed with Neilson's name.[43]

Madame de Pompadour's furniture must have been very similar to her brother's, but Jacques did not mention the "ornemens" (ornaments), presumably the scrolling forms most conspicuous at the bottom of the designs of the examples listed above. Madame de Pompadour's unmounted pieces had been paid for, according to Marigny's letter, so they may or may not have been returned to the factory, later to become part of another set. Although it is uncertain whether any of the existing pieces of upholstery were

made for her or her brother, it is conceivable that their furniture has survived. As Pierre Verlet, the great expert on French decorative art, used to say, "Everything exists."

Madame de Pompadour first commissioned a set of tapestry furniture covers as early as 1751;[44] she has even been credited with establishing the fashion for Gobelins upholstery. Tapestry furniture covers had been made at Beauvais since at least the 1690s, but only very occasionally at the Gobelins before Madame de Pompadour's first set.[45]

Some covers for the 1751 set of Madame de Pompadour's furniture had been finished by 8 May 1752, when her brother wrote a peremptory letter to Garnier d'Isle:

Aussitost que vous aurés receu ma lettre, Monsieur, vous aurés agréable de dire à M. Neilson qu'il remette à M. Boucher les tableaux qu'il à fait et d'après lesquels le Sr Neilson a fait les fauteuils de Made la Marquise de Pompadour, et qu'à l'avenir, il les luy remette tout de suite et immédiatement après que les fonds ou le dossier du fauteuil sera achevé et oté du dessus le metier.[46]

On 25 May he wrote again, even more forcibly, saying that Madame de Pompadour absolutely forbade Neilson to make more covers after these designs and that she wished the weaver to turn over to Garnier d'Isle "toutes les copies qu'il a tirées d'après les originaux de M. Boucher, du moment même que chaque qui est sur le métier en sera demonté."[47] Vandières, on a visit to the Gobelins, was told by Neilson that the weaver was keeping the copies to make tapestries from them for "particuliers" (private customers). Neilson may have suggested this as a good way to raise money, both for himself and for the always hard-pressed manufactory, but he had to eat his words. Garnier d'Isle was quick to reply to Vandières, on 28 May, that the weaver had painted a copy of Boucher's design merely to show the directeur "son ouvrage en peinture, et vous faire, par là, sa cour"[48]; he had already given back eight designs for sidechairs and four for bergères (armchairs with side panels).

These documents indicate that the set contained armchairs, sidechairs, and bergères, so that it is presumably the one recorded in Madame de Pompadour's inventory as found in the "grand Salon" of her house in Paris:

Quatre fauteuils, un canapé de trois places, deux fauteuils en bergère, et trois chaises [one must have been missing, as Boucher had made eight designs for backs and seats], le tout garny de crin, couvert de tapisserie des Gobelins, dessins de M. Boucher représentant des enfants.[49]

The twenty Boucher designs mentioned in Garnier d'Isle's letter of 28 May would be sufficient for this furniture, with a sofa added. The inventory also lists an écran (firescreen) "garny de son feuille de même tapisserie"[50] and a paravent (tall screen) "de six feuilles à bois doré de tapisserie des Gobelins, représentant des jeux d'enfants d'un cotté, et des fleurs et fables de l'autre."[51]

This furniture may have been used at Bellevue. Later, Madame de Pompadour wanted more. Garnier d'Isle wrote to her brother on 2 May 1755 about a set that Neilson was making for her; it was to include covers for two very large sofas, fourteen pieds long, which could not be finished before the beginning of 1756, but eight armchairs and a firescreen were half done and would be ready by the end of the year. Garnier d'Isle's successor, Soufflot,

wrote to Marigny on 16 February 1756 that the furniture covers would be delivered at the end of April.[52] Nothing more is known of this set, unless part of it was in a salon of the chateau of Menars, which Madame de Pompadour had bought in 1760. The description of this furniture in Madame de Pompadour's inventory reads:

Deux canapés à trois places et six chaises à bois doré, garnis de crin, couvert de tapisserie des Gobelins, représentant les Arts et autres sujets, avec leurs housses de toile grise, et un écran, aussy à bois doré, garni de sa feuille de tapisserie des Gobelins.[53]

The sofas, however, do not seem to be long enough to measure fourteen feet, and Garnier d'Isle's letter refers to eight armchairs, not sidechairs. Boucher's name is not associated with the Menars set, but the mention of Arts as the subjects makes his authorship of the designs almost certain; no other artist was supplying the Gobelins with small figures at this time.

The Arts, personified as children in Boucher's style, are, in fact, found on a number of Gobelins furniture covers. There are three types. Nude winged pairs of putti, or babies, are on the backs of five armchairs in the Huntington Collection, San Marino, California; they represent Music (two chairs), Drawing, Architecture, and perhaps Astronomy (one putto lighting his torch with a burning glass, the other putto looking through a telescope, fig. 18). Two sofa-backs in the same set show groups of similar putti, on one panel shooting arrows at a target, on the other, playing by a fountain.[54] Modèles for one sofa-back, one Music, Architecture, Astronomy, and Drawing are in the Mobilier National, Paris, with a comparable one for Sculpture, of which no tapestry has been located.[55]

The compositions usually called the Enfants de Boucher are a second type, very well known, as a number of them were also used as models for porcelain figurines. The largest published set of the furniture covers belonged to George A. Cooper in 1903[56] and was sold at Christie's on 1 December 1966, no. 95, by the Trustees of the Hursley Settlement. It consists of a sofa (6 ft. 4½ in. wide), two bergères (one with Neilson's name), six

18. Weavers of the Gobelins Manufactory after François Boucher, *Astronomy*, c. 1760–1770, wool and silk tapestry, 46 x 40 (18 x 16)
The Henry E. Huntington Library and Art Gallery, San Marino

19. Workshop of Jacques Neilson at the Gobelins Manufactory after François Boucher, *Girl Feeding Chickens*, 1750–1788, wool and silk tapestry, 71.5 x 52.2 (28 x 21)
The Metropolitan Museum of Art, Gift of Barbara Weisl in loving memory of Rowene and James Seligman, 1986

20. Weavers of the Gobelins Manufactory after François Boucher, *Poetry*, c. 1760–1770, wool and silk tapestry, 46 x 40 (18 x 16)
The Henry E. Huntington Library and Art Gallery, San Marino

armchairs, and a firescreen. Several other sets and individual pieces are known. Among these, the upholstery for six armchairs and a firescreen in the Rijksmuseum, Amsterdam, can be given an approximate date of 1751–1752, as it was originally used on English frames commissioned at that time.[57] These *Enfants* are young children, not babies, in simplified contemporary dress. Most of them are single figures in landscapes, sometimes engaged in an activity such as fishing, dancing, eating, playing the bagpipe, making a wreath, or feeding chickens (fig. 19). At least eighteen different figures are known, more girls than boys. The sofas associated with the chairs have children in pairs imitating typical Boucher pastimes for adults, such as the boy teaching a girl to play the flute. Several *modèles* are in the Mobilier National and elsewhere.[58]

Finally, there are the entrancing, fully clothed small people, a little younger than the *Enfants de Boucher* but older than the putti, who are actively practicing an art or some branch of science, or, in rarer instances, personifying one. They adorn the backs of five armchairs in the Huntington Collection;[59] one from a different set is on an armchair in the Fine Arts Museums of San Francisco and another is in the Residenz, Munich.[60] The small people are working at painting and sculpture, writing poetry (fig. 20), and posing with the attrib-

jets." Of the sets known today, five pieces owned by the San Francisco Museums (four chairs and a sofa) and twelve (ten armchairs and two sofas) in the Huntington Collection have been associated with Madame de Pompadour, but there is no firm evidence in either case.[62]

One is left to conjecture as to which type of Boucher designs for furniture covers are more likely to have been used for Madame de Pompadour's orders. She owned porcelain figurines of the *Enfants de Boucher* and might have wanted them on her chairs as well. It was the designs with children after Boucher, however, commissioned for upholstery in 1751, that Madame de Pompadour insisted were not to be woven for anyone else. This prohibition must certainly have lasted until her death in 1764, but one set of the standard *Enfants de Boucher*, as previously noted, is known to date from the early 1750s.

Both the series of winged putti and the series with youngsters like those on the Frick panels could be described as "children" or as representing the arts and other subjects. The putti would have been in keeping not only with the figures in Madame de Pompadour's *Génies* tapestries but also with the prints that she made herself, some of them after Boucher, that show mostly nude children.[63] However, the children like those on the Frick panels would seem to have the closest connection with her. The paintings are said to have come from a boudoir in her chateau of Crécy, whose decoration was completed in 1751. It might be argued that the necessarily somewhat coarser versions for upholstery in wool and silk would have been unappealing compared to the more brilliant and subtle paintings on the walls. But Madame de Pompadour owned both the *Apollo* paintings and the tapestries copied from them, so there is nothing inherently improbable in the idea that the figures on the walls of her boudoir should reappear on her furniture. It may also be significant that some *modèles* for the putti and the *Enfants de Boucher* are still at the Gobelins manufactory, whereas there are no separate paintings of the Frick subjects there; this

utes of Comedy (fig. 21). They are reproductions, though not exact copies, in wool and silk, of some of the figures on the set of wall paintings by Boucher in the Frick Collection, New York.[61]

To sum up, Madame de Pompadour's sets of furniture in Gobelins upholstery with figures included one set of ten armchairs, a three-seat sofa, a firescreen, and a six-panel tall screen; the designs were children after Boucher, who was responsible for both backs and seats. A second set, according to one document, had two very long sofas, eight armchairs, and a firescreen; according to another document (unless, indeed, a third set is being described), it consisted of two three-seat sofas, six sidechairs, and a firescreen, with representations of "les *Arts* et autre su-

suggests that it was the *modèles* of the Frick type that were returned to Boucher.[64]

Madame de Pompadour cannot be called an innovator where tapestry is concerned, although her commissions indicate her continuing patronage of Boucher; without these tapestry designs, his work for the Gobelins would have been very scanty. Her orders and prompt payments, especially during the difficult time of the Seven Years War (1756–1763), must have been very welcome at the manufactory.[65] Her fondness for tapestry upholstery would seem to have inspired the happy concept of entire rooms hung and furnished with Gobelins weavings, which resulted in such masterpieces as the Tapestry Rooms at Croome Court, with Jacques' flowers on the furniture, now at the Metropolitan Museum of Art, and at Osterley Park near London, where the furniture has the *Enfants de Boucher*. Even as late as 1783, nearly twenty years after Madame de Pompadour's last commission, Jacques' flowers were reproduced on the furniture now at Welbeck Abbey in Nottinghamshire. Her patronage did indeed have lasting importance for the Gobelins manufactory.

NOTES

All translations from French are by the author.

1. The Gobelins records have been magnificently published in Maurice Fenaille, *Etat général des tapisseries de la manufacture des Gobelins depuis son origine jusqu'à nos jours, 1600–1900*, 6 vols. (Paris, 1903–1923).

2. Jean Cordey, *Inventaire des biens de Madame de Pompadour rédigé après son décès* (Paris, 1939). Listed in addition to Gobelins tapestries are Aubusson "tapis de pied" (foot carpets) and Aubusson upholstery for a *canapé* (sofa), *fauteuils* (armchairs), *banquettes* (benches), and *tabourets* (stools), appraised for very small sums, but no Aubusson wall hangings and no Beauvais tapestries.

3. Emile Campardon, *Madame de Pompadour et la Cour de Louis xv au milieu du dix-huitième siècle* (Paris, 1867), 333–357.

4. For an account of tapestry or tapestries after Van Ostade, see Fenaille 4, 1907, 338–339. [The upright-loom tapestry after the original by Ostade, presented to the king by monsieur the director general.]

5. A woman holding a child and leaning on her door; this piece is made in petit-point embroidery by Neilson at the Gobelins, after Adriaen van Ostade, glazed and in a gilded frame.

6. A subject, excellently carried out, in tapestry, by Sieur Cozette, at the Royal Manufactory of the Gobelins, representing a Dutch woman holding her child in her arms and leaning on the lower part of the door of her house. The capital picture of this master has been part of the celebrated collection owned by the duke of Choiseul. This piece is glazed and is 39 inches by 30 inches in length.

7. *Recueil d'estampes gravées d'après les tableaux du cabinet de Monseigneur le duc de Choiseul par les soins de Sr Basan* MDCCLXXI. *A Paris chès l'auteur*, no. 15.

8. Campardon 1867, 333. [The greater part of the items in the present catalogue come from the estate of Madame the Marquise de Pompadour.]

9. Campardon 1867, 337, no. 24.

10. Fenaille 4, 1907, 343–344.

11. Fenaille 3, 1904, 15.

12. Fenaille 4, 1907, 173–182, gives a history of the two tapestries from which most of the following account has been taken. [Madame the Marquise having had the goodness to turn her eyes upon me to make her two pieces after M. Boucher intended for Bellevue, of which the first panel should be finished by the end of this month.]

13. John Ingamells, *The Wallace Collection Catalogue of Pictures* III, *French before 1815* (London, 1989), nos. P485–P486.

14. Campardon 1867, 321, no. 14 in the sale of 28 April 1766.

15. The piece after M. Boucher, which I have the honor of executing in tapestry for Madame your sister.

16. Edith A. Standen, "Tapestries in Use: Indoors," *Apollo* 113 (1981), fig. 13.

17. Jean Mondain-Monval, *Correspondance de Soufflot avec les Directeurs des Bâtiments concernant la manufacture des Gobelins 1756–1780* (Paris, 1918), 62–63. [You know, Sir, the two pieces of tapestry that my sister had made at the Gobelins after Boucher's designs. They fitted the place where they were hung at Bellevue. Today it is necessary to enlarge them with a border for the new place that has been arranged for them. My sister wishes these borders to be made by M. Boucher and that they

should be related to the subject of the tapestries; arrange this with M. Boucher and M. Cozette and send me a written answer that I can show my sister.]

18. Mondain-Monval 1918, 62–63. [Sir, in the last few days, I have been at the Hôtel de Pompadour to verify the measurements that were given me by M. le Queustre; examining the place where the two pieces of tapestry after M. Boucher's paintings are to be hung, I have seen that the borders they will need to fill the space should be eighteen to nineteen inches in width; I have since arranged with M. Boucher to go to the Gobelins today to examine the various borders of the manufactory there; we spent the morning there and agreed there on the type of the ones you ordered; as the matter is one of ornament and as Sieur Jacques paints this very well, M. Boucher has given his ideas, and I the measurements, so that he can make a sketch, from which he will make the paintings for the execution, during this time the canvases will be prepared, so that Mme the Marquise can be promptly satisfied; to paint the borders more naturalistically, we thought it would be good to look at the real thing, and as there are, Sir, very beautiful gilded wooden frames in the Luxembourg storehouse, I visited M. Bailly to ask him to send some of them, which will be afterwards returned, to M. Belle and M. Boucher, who should make their choice this afternoon; the borders that will be made after them will imitate the gilding better, and they will be enriched with the attributes of Apollo, the flowers and fruits which he makes grow, and branches of coral and other products of the sea that are seen in the two subjects.]

19. Mondain-Monval 1918, 62–63. [You have seen on the looms at the Royal Manufactory of the Gobelins the borders that are being made there for Madame the Marquise de Pompadour, she has paid for the tracings for them taken from the paintings by M. Boizot and which M. Cozette needed for the execution; as these paintings are substantial and rich in flowers and ornaments very carefully carried out, they could be useful for a long time on work done for the King, for this reason I think, Sir, that they should be paid for by the Bâtiments; they have occupied M. Jacques for a long time; he has zealously followed M. Boucher's advice and has made with pleasure any alterations that he wanted while the work was in progress.]

20. Fenaille 4, 1907, fig. facing p. 180.

21. Fresher than the pieces.

22. Have lost much of their freshness.

23. Fenaille 2, 1903, 355–356, 370.

24. *Memoires du Duc de Luynes sur la cour de Louis xv* (Paris, 1883), 13, 442. This set could not have been the *Enfants jardiniers* or the *Métamorphoses*, which were not owned by the marquise until 1760–1761. [There is actually a Gobelins tapestry set into the paneling in the large salon. In the middle of these tapestry panels there are two capital Ls under a crown.]

25. Fenaille 2, 1903, 69, 84, 89.

26. Fenaille 2, 1903, 92–95; Cordey 1939, 154 (no. 1908, four pieces), 172 (no. 2108).

27. Fenaille 3, 1906, 129–130.

28. Edith A. Standen, "Ovid's *Métamorphoses*: A Gobelins Tapestry Series," *Metropolitan Museum Journal* 23 (1988), 149–191.

29. Cordey 1939, 162 (no. 1988), 172 (no. 2108). In the first room, the height of the tapestries is given as three *aunes* (ells), whereas the *Métamorphoses* when woven were only 2 14/16 *aunes* high, but the difference is not great (1 *aune*=1.18 m).

30. Fenaille 4, 1907, 189–207, provides an account of the series and of the first two sets, woven for Marigny and Madame de Pompadour.

31. To make it large enough for the piece ordered by Madame the Marquise de Pompadour.

32. Fenaille 4, 1907, 206. [Twelve and three sixteenths and a quarter of horizontal-loom tapestry, made at the Gobelins, representing the *Génies des Arts* and subjects of the *Amours des dieux*.]

33. You must try, Soufflot, to sell to an Englishman or someone else the tapestries that my sister has ordered at the Gobelins and that she has paid for. I want you to put into this all the zeal and energy that you devote to things of interest to me.

34. Other examples have been cited by Heinrich Gobel, *Wandteppiche II. Die romanischen Länder* (Leipzig, 1928), 1, 185; 2, fig. 175 (Griffin piece, then owned by the dealers French & Co.). The author lists what he describes as the fragment of another weaving illustrated in Hermann Schmitz, *Bildteppiche, Geschichte der Gobelinwirkerei* (Berlin, 1919), 302, fig. 152, but this is actually a detail of the Griffin example. George Leland Hunter, *The Practical Book of Tapestries* (Philadelphia and New York, 1925), 189, mentions, but does not illustrate, an example owned by the dealer Jacques Seligmann.

35. Fenaille 4, 1907, fig. facing p. 196.

36. I have asked M. Neilson for a bluish white background that, I believe, will make the flowers stand out and will be in keeping with the woodwork of the room, which is to have a varnished white ground with gilded moldings, like the frames of the armchairs.

37. Ten paintings designed and diversified with different masses of flowers, with borders of ornaments interlaced with little flowers and ten more small paintings for the armrests. . . . Two paintings, one of 6½ feet, the other of 7½ feet, adorned with flowers and a border of designed ornaments similar to the paintings mentioned above, and two small paintings for the armrests.

38. Fenaille 4, 1907, 389–390, 392–393, gives an account of upholstery after Jacques made for Marigny and Madame de Pompadour. [Twenty designs for armchairs, both seats and backs, painted and colored in gouache, showing different groups of

flowers enclosed in a little border of flowers to mark the edge.]

39. Cordey 1939, 141, nos. 1826–1829. [The covers of ten complete armchairs with flowers and ornaments, white and red ground. . . . The covers of two sofas of 7 feet 6 inches long by 3 feet 6 inches deep, one without a back. . . . A screen of six leaves of similar Gobelins tapestry. . . . A little firescreen.]

40. Edith A. Standen, *European Post-Medieval Tapestries and Related Hangings in The Metropolitan Museum of Art* (New York, 1985), 396–398.

41. Alfred Marquiset, *Le Marquis de Marigny, 1727–1781* (Paris, 1918), 113.

42. Standen 1985, 1, 402–404, fig. 43. The account of the *modèles* in the Mobilier National is not accurate; in addition to the one illustrated, *modèles* for the second Metropolitan Museum panel, a sofa-back and seat, another chair-back and four chair-seats of the series have been published (Jules Guiffrey, *Les Modèles et le Musée des Gobelins* [Paris, n.d.], figs. 47, 49–53. All are attributed to Louis Tessier].

43. Standen 1985, 1, 404. To the examples listed can be added two panels mounted as screens, but most probably chair-backs, owned in 1987 by the London dealer Norman Adams, Ltd. The screen listed as last sold at Sotheby's, London, 21 June 1977, no. 6, was sold again at the Nouveau Drouot, Paris, 16 June 1987, no. 191.

44. Fenaille 4, 1907, 384–388, gives an account of the first upholstery set made for Madame de Pompadour.

45. Fenaille 4, 1907, 377. Furniture covers were added to the set of *Don Quixote* Gobelins tapestries given by the king to Count Vorontzov in 1759, and the first designs for upholstery with flowers on simulated damask grounds were recorded in 1760 (Fenaille 4, 1907, 391, 394; Standen 1985, 1, 374, 396–399). Admiration for such upholstery is indicated by the inclusion of "fauteuils des Gobelins et d'étoffes" (armchairs with Gobelins and fabrics) in the publication *Annonces, affiches et avis divers* for that year (quoted in Pierre Rosenberg and Jacques Thuillier, *Laurent de La Hyre* [exh. cat., Grenoble, 1988]), 292.

46. As soon as you receive my letter, Sir, be good enough to tell M. Neilson to return to M. Boucher the paintings that he has made after which Sieur Neilson has made Madame de Pompadour's armchairs, and that in the future he will return them at once and immediately when the seat or the back of the armchair has been finished and taken from the loom.

47. All the copies that he has made after M. Boucher's originals, the very moment when each one comes off the loom.

48. His work as a painter, and pay his court to you in this way.

49. Four armchairs, a sofa of three places, two armchairs of the *bergère* type, and three sidechairs, all furnished with horsehair, covered with Gobelins tapestry with designs of children by M. Boucher.

50. Furnished with its leaf of the same tapestry.

51. Cordey 1939, 26. The entry shows that designs of *Fables* (usually associated with Beauvais) were woven at the Gobelins. [Of six leaves in gilded wood of Gobelins tapestry, representing children's games on one side and flowers and fables on the other.]

52. Fenaille 4, 1907, 388.

53. Cordey 1939, 154. [Two sofas of three places and six sidechairs of gilded wood, furnished with horsehair, covered with Gobelins tapestry representing the arts and other subjects, with their slipcovers of gray linen, and a screen, also of gilded wood, furnished with its leaf of Gobelins tapestry.]

54. Robert R. Wark, *French Decorative Art in the Huntington Collection* (San Marino, 1961), 71–72, figs. 22–27. Fig. 22 (*Music*) shows only a single putto, but another tapestry version of the design has a second child above the helmet on the left (Alexandre Ananoff, *François Boucher* [Lausanne-Paris, 1976], 2, 127, no. 444/1, fig. 1257, as in the Daniel Wildenstein Collection). The Huntington tapestry shows no sign of having been altered, so the change must have been made in the cartoon.

55. Ananoff 1976, 2, nos. 442, 444–448. The author lists all the *modèles* as belonging to the Beauvais manufactory before coming to the Gobelins but gives no source for this information.

56. Francis Bennett Goldney, *Some Works of Art in the Possession of George A. Cooper at 26 Grosvenor Square* (London, 1903), 14–23.

57. William Rieder, "Eighteenth-Century Chairs in the Untermyer Collection," *Apollo* 107 (1978), 184. The author describes the chairs as "obviously specifically designed to carry the Gobelins coverings."

58. Ananoff 1976, 2, nos. 438–443, 449–450.

59. Wark 1961, figs. 16–17, 20–21, 29.

60. Anna Gray Bennett, *Five Centuries of Tapestries in the Fine Arts Museums of San Francisco*, rev. ed. (San Francisco, 1992), no. 90, 286.

61. *The Frick Collection* (Pittsburgh, 1949), 1, 149–157.

62. The San Francisco chairs have four figures resembling the Frick panels, and the Huntington set has five of this type and seven with putti, counting the two sofas. The date 1779 is recorded as having been found on one Huntington chair cover, too late for the set to have been made for Madame de Pompadour (Wark 1961, 72). Though the tapestries show two types of Boucher children, all have the same twisted ribbon borders. The oval chair-backs are of a later type than those of the San Francisco oblongs with slight curves of the chairs, which are in the Louis xv style and quite possibly are from Madame de Pompadour's set. The Munich tapestry is on an original but later frame.

63. Albert de La Fizelière, "L'Art et les femmes en France. Madame de Pompadour," *Gazette des Beaux-Arts* 3 (1859), 129–152.

64. It has been suggested that the Frick paintings were cartoons for Bellevue furniture covers before they were used at the chateau of Crécy. See Jean Bastien, "Le roi chez Madame de Pompadour et la floraison des arts" [exh. cat., David M. Stewart Museum] (Montreal, 1988), 88, 94. The Frick paintings show no signs of having served as tapestry cartoons, and the chair-backs with similar designs are sufficiently different from them to cast doubt on the possibility. M. Bastien has said in a private letter that he will publish documentation for his claim.

65. The budget of the Bâtiments in 1763 was only half what it had been earlier (Marquiset 1918, 114). Madame de Pompadour's promptness in settling her accounts with the manufactory is indicated by Marigny's statement that she had already paid for the tapestry being made for her at the time of her death. Her concern for the well-being of both the Gobelins and the Savonnerie establishments is shown in a letter supporting her brother's appeal for financial assistance for them (Pierre de Nolhac, *Louis xv et Madame de Pompadour*, 1903, 135). For an authoritative account of her patronage as a whole, see Donald Posner, "Mme de Pompadour as a Patron of the Visual Arts," *The Art Bulletin* 72 (1990), 74–105.

CANDACE ADELSON

Apollo and Daphne *from Charles de La Fosse's* Ovid's Fables

A Series Designed for the Leyniers-Reydams Workshop in Brussels

In 1951 the Honorable Lewis Einstein gave a tapestry representing the myth of *Apollo and Daphne* to the National Gallery of Art, Washington (fig. 1).[1] H. C. Marillier, who knew the tapestry in Einstein's collection in London before World War II, thought that it had been woven either in Brussels or at the Gobelins in Paris.[2] Einstein had received conflicting opinions that it was either a Beauvais or a Gobelins piece, woven in the eighteenth century. At the time it entered the National Gallery, Mitchell Samuels of French and Company attributed the tapestry to Brussels and dated it about 1700–1710. Later, both Madeleine Jarry and Adolph S. Cavallo essentially agreed with this assessment.[3]

When I was asked to write about the National Gallery of Art's tapestries and textiles for their systematic catalogue in 1984,[4] *Apollo and Daphne* was one of the few pieces not on display. On the basis of the black-and-white photograph, an early eighteenth-century date for this tapestry, agreed on by the majority of experts, seemed plausible, but the design did indeed have both French and Flemish elements. Consequently I anticipated seeing the piece with great curiosity. How clearly I remember unrolling it with Joe Columbus in his laboratory, and the thrill we felt as the incredibly well-preserved, brilliant, and quite obviously Flemish colors came to light. Together we spent quite some time reveling in the fine weaving and deft modeling. It was one of the most exhilarating of the many bright moments I recall passing with Joe, and one I am therefore pleased to share with others as we honor him at this symposium.

Attribution

The superlative design and execution of *Apollo and Daphne* could only indicate a major Brussels atelier, working from the cartoon of a master painter. Marillier had recognized another tapestry with this composition (fig. 2). Its present location is unknown.[5] It has a border of the type called *bastons rompus*, used briefly by the Beauvais manufactory beginning in the late seventeenth century. The figures of Daphne and the water nymph are now missing, and the tapestry has been recomposed around the missing areas like a jigsaw puzzle. Since there is no evidence this border was imitated in Brussels, and as far as is known the composition was not woven in France, it is probable that the border is not original and was attached when the piece was cut down.[6]

Ingrid De Meûter, when consulted about the National Gallery of Art's tapestry, thought it was probably by the large Brussels workshop jointly operated by

fig. 1 (detail)

1. Atelier of Urban and Daniel II Leyniers and Henry II Reydams, Brussels, after a cartoon by Charles de La Fosse, *Apollo and Daphne*, from the *Ovid's Fables* series, 1714–1715, tapestry, 359.4 x 413.1 (149¼ x 172⅛)
National Gallery of Art, Washington, no. 1951.1.1

2. Atelier of Urban and Daniel II Leyniers and Henry II Reydams, Brussels, after a cartoon by Charles de La Fosse, *Apollo and Daphne*, from the *Ovid's Fables* series, 1714–1721, tapestry, 292.1 x 299.7 (115 x 118), fragmentary, border not original
Present location unknown. Photo courtesy Trustees of the Victoria and Albert Museum

3. Atelier of Urban and Daniel II Leyniers and Henry II Reydams, Brussels, after a cartoon by Victor Janssens, *Theseus Dancing before the Great Temple of Apollo on the Island of Delos*, from the *Famous Men after Plutarch* series, 1712–1719, tapestry, 380 x 450 (153 x 178)
Present location unknown. Photo courtesy Sotheby's

4. Charles de La Fosse, *Young Woman with Dark Hair*, c. 1712–1714, pastel on blue paper, 28 x 23.9 (11 x 9½) Nationalmuseum, Stockholm

5. Head of a naiad, detail of fig. 1

Urban (1674–1747) and Daniel II (1669–1728) Leyniers and Henry II Reydams (1650–1719), because there are identical fictive picture-frame borders on a signed set of *Famous Men after Plutarch* (fig. 3).[7] According to contemporary records, the firm wove three sets of a series called *Ovid's Fables* from cartoons by the great Parisian painter Charles de La Fosse (1636–1716).[8] De Meûter suggested that *Apollo and Daphne* might be from this series, which included a piece called *Daphne*. However, no pieces of *Ovid's Fables* had yet been identified, and the firm had at least one other mythological series in its repertory.[9]

Confirmation of De Meûter's hypothesis can be found in two pastel studies traditionally attributed to Charles de La Fosse, which were in fact used for the tapestry. One is for the head of the naiad and is reversed in respect to the final weaving (figs. 4 and 5). It is one of a group of La Fosse pastel studies in Stockholm.[10] The other, in the Louvre, is for the head of Daphne and faces in the same direction as the head of the figure in the tapestry (figs. 6 and 7).[11]

The tapestry's style also compares convincingly with La Fosse's paintings. From as early as 1688–1689, when he worked for the Trianon de Marbre at Versailles, La Fosse created narrative compositions with a limited number of figures; the movements and drapery style of the tapestry's figures have their closest parallels, however, in his late mythological paintings from about 1700 or later.[12] The composition is not the same as that of La Fosse's one identified painting of *Apollo Pursuing Daphne* in Orléans. Apollo, however, resembles in type the *Apollo on His Chariot* in the Salle d'Apollon at Versailles.[13]

The La Fosse/Leyniers-Reydams *Ovid's Fables* Series

The first set of the Leyniers-Reydams *Ovid's Fables* was woven in 1714 for the Brussels palace of the dowager duchess of Arenberg; the records do not give its subjects and dimensions. In 1715 six more were sent to Vienna to Imperial Treasurer-General van Ysendyck, who had specified the dimensions required. The subjects of the pieces were Diana, Europa, Daphne,

6. Charles de La Fosse, *Portrait of a Young Woman,* c. 1712–1714, pastel on gray paper, 32.3 x 26.4 (12¾ x 10⅓) Département des Arts Graphiques, Musée du Louvre, Paris, ©R. M. N.

7. Daphne's head, detail of fig. 1

"La Nymphe près d'Apollon" (the nymph and/with Apollo), "Polipkin" (Polyphemus), and Arethusa. In 1721 the firm sent to the dowager de Wassenaer in The Hague—via the Dutch Resident Pester—a third, five-piece set, which was 4¾ ells high (3.31 m; 10 ft. 10⅜ in.) and 22½ ells (15.69 m; 51 ft. 5¹¹⁄₁₆ in.) in total length. No other sets are documented.[14] The National Gallery of Art's tapestry is 28 cm (11 in.) higher than the third set, so it probably belonged to one of the two earlier sets; its completion can thus be dated c. 1714–1715.

It appears, then, that La Fosse's six Ovidian designs for the series were *Diana, The Story of Europa, Apollo and Daphne, The Nymph and Apollo, Polyphemus,* and *Alpheus and Arethusa.* On the basis of *Apollo and Daphne,* three of the other designs for this series can now also be identified.

The composition entitled "Diana" in 1715, better known as *Diana's Return from the Hunt* (fig. 8), represents Diana resting after the hunt, while one of her nymphs loosens the goddess' sandals in preparation for her bath. As Edith Standen has demonstrated, it was among La Fosse's most successful compositions. The docu-

mented painted versions include a large canvas in the Hermitage, a lost one painted for the Trianon in 1688–1689, and another that was engraved by Pierre-Etienne Moitte in 1754, as well as two smaller pictures showing only the central figures, presently in the Art Gallery of Ontario, Toronto (fig. 9), and the Musée des Beaux-Arts, Rennes. There are also two known tapestry variants. By 1715, but probably as early as 1705, the composition was copied from a La Fosse painting similar to the Hermitage canvas for use in the Gobelins series of Ovid's *Metamorphoses;* it became one of the most popular subjects of that series.[15]

The second tapestry version of this design was woven in Brussels. Its central group is closest to the Toronto painting (fig. 9), but the side figures and landscape are different from any other variant. One of the three known tapestries of this version is signed by the Leyniers-Reydams firm (see fig. 8). Another is the companion to a *Europa and the Bull* in La Fosse's style, signed by Urban Leyniers (fig. 10).[16] Since the *Ovid's Fables* series also included a story of Europa, it seems that this latter pair of tapestries is from one of the sets of the series woven in the

painted precursors were apparently designed to emphasize the derivation from Ovid's description, and thus adapt the design more closely for use in an entire series based on the *Metamorphoses*. As Kalf points out, the motif of the nymph removing Diana's sandals for her bath after the hunt, already present in La Fosse's first versions of the story, derives from Ovid.[17] To stress the ancient literary source even further, however, at the left of the new tapestry design the artist added the natural rock arch in the vale of Gargaphie described by Ovid, near which Diana liked to bathe.[18]

The first known *Diana* tapestry is now 26 cm (10¼ in.) shorter in height than the set delivered to the dowager de Wassenaer in 1721, and its border design is an example of a second fictive frame type used for this series. The second *Diana* tapestry, in still another border, is the same height as the de Wassenaer tapestries and may well be from this set. By this time Henry II Reydams was dead, which might explain why only Urban Leyniers' name appears on the signed companion piece.[19] The third known Brussels tapestry of the composition, signed by Frans Van der Borght, seems to have been woven from the same cartoon and is probably the latest in

Leyniers-Reydams shop, and therefore that this *Diana* composition must be the one habitually used in the series. In fact, the changes made in evolving it from its

date.[20] Frans' relative, Peter Van der Borght, apparently also used the composition to represent Diana in a series of *Triumphs of the Gods*. The Van der Borght family may have acquired the cartoon after the Leyniers shop no longer had any use for it.[21]

As noted above, the tapestry called "Europa" in the records was a *Europa and the Bull*. The one example thus far identified is from the same set as one of the known *Diana* weavings, a set that was probably originally owned by the dowager de Wassenaer (fig. 10a). It is signed in the main composition at the lower left "U. LEYNIERS"(fig. 10b), and shows Jupiter metamorphosed into a docile bull with Europa on his back, just before he carries her off.[22] Though documents record that La Fosse also depicted the *Rape of Europa* in painting, this tapestry is his only surviving version of the theme presently known. A large La Fosse figure study of a woman with

nude torso may be a preliminary study for Europa; it is in mirror image to the tapestry.[23] Among the La Fosse pastel studies in Stockholm, one of a *Girl with Streaming Hair Gazing Upward* may have served as a model for Europa's head; it is also in the opposite direction from the tapestry.[24]

The fourth identifiable La Fosse design for *Ovid's Fables* is known from a tapestry with identical borders, stylistically similar

10a. Atelier of Urban and Daniel II Leyniers, Brussels, after a cartoon by Charles de La Fosse, *Europa and the Bull*, 1721(?), tapestry, 330 x 530 (130 x 208⅔) Luciano Coen, Rome

10b. Detail

11. Here attributed to the atelier of Urban and Daniel II Leyniers and Henry II Reydams, Brussels, after a cartoon by Charles de La Fosse, *The Nymph and Apollo (Apollo and Tethys?)*, from the *Ovid's Fables* series, 1714–1715, tapestry, 381 x 388.6 (150 x 153) Present location unknown. Photo courtesy Trustees of the Victoria and Albert Museum

to the Gallery's *Apollo and Daphne*. Auctioned in 1934, it measured 22 cm higher than the Gallery's piece. Only a tiny partial photograph is known (fig. 11). The scene was catalogued as "a Muse making an offering to Apollo surrounded by six other figures, in a landscape," and plausibly corresponds to the composition called *The Nymph and Apollo* in the *Ovid's Fables* set of 1715. To Marillier, the offering appeared to be a handful of pearls.[25] The subject is unclear. It may be the ocean goddess Tethys offering the riches of the sea to Apollo. *Apollo and Tethys* was a popular theme in the imagery that adulated Louis XIV of France in the seventeenth century, derived in part from a verse in Ovid.[26] La Fosse had painted it for the Trianon de Marbre in 1688–1689.[27] On the other hand, there is a child with a whistle and mask behind the nymph, and a woman appears to be sneaking up behind Apollo. This may indicate that the nymph is a decoy to distract him. Such a scene does not seem to derive from common mythological sources and could perhaps have come from contemporary theater.

There are as yet few indications as to the designs of La Fosse's remaining two

compositions for the *Ovid's Fables* series. As noted above, the *Diana* of this series is based on a La Fosse composition that had probably already been marked for use in tapestries by the time the Leyniers-Reydams series was designed. For one other subject La Fosse and the Leyniers-Reydams firm had the possibility of reusing a design already chosen by the Gobelins. The scene called "Polipkin" most likely refers to the story of the one-eyed giant Polyphemus, who was enamored of the nymph Galatea who in turn loved the youth Acis. La Fosse especially liked the story, perhaps because of the range of figure types and expressions it afforded, and depicted it a number of times. By 1684, two of his paintings were copied by the Gobelins and enlarged into two distinct tapestry cartoons, both titled *Acis and Galatea* (figs. 12 and 13), for the same *Metamorphoses* series as *Diana's Return from the Hunt*.[28] Therefore, the title "Polipkin" might possibly designate a composition similar to one or the other. Since, as noted, La Fosse is known to have painted at least one *Rape of Europa*, as well as an *Apollo and Tethys*, of the six *Ovid's Fables* subjects, only *Alpheus and Arethusa* may have been new to him.[29] As far as can be known at the present point in La Fosse studies, however, it seems he did not always reuse his earlier inventions for the *Ovid's Fables* tapestries, as he did for *Diana's Return from the Hunt*, but may have taken advantage of this unique opportunity to design new compositions. This appears to be the case for *Apollo and Daphne, The Nymph and Apollo (Apollo and Tethys?)*, and *Alpheus and Arethusa*.

The central figures of these tapestries are all close to La Fosse in style. Urban Leyniers, who maintained the workshop's correspondence and client relations, made at least seventeen trips to Paris in twenty-two years, so the firm must have had direct contacts with the painter. This is further confirmed by the new compositions La Fosse apparently created for the series. Moreover, the sparkling tonalities and patently La Fosse modeling in the National Gallery of Art's *Apollo and Daphne* indicate the painter's personal participation in the cartoons, at least in the

figures.[30] The landscape compositions of the four known *Ovid's Fables* designs also appear to be by La Fosse; however, the Flemish style of the vegetation suggests that the details were left for Brussels specialists. It was then common practice for a figure painter and a landscape painter to collaborate on tapestry cartoons, and La Fosse is known to have followed this procedure even in paintings. The vegetation in *Apollo and Daphne* is particularly close to that in a *Neptune* tapestry (fig. 14) from the Leyniers-Reydams *Triumphs of the Gods,* with cartoons that had figures by Jan Van Orley and landscapes by Augustin Coppens. Coppens, a regular Leyniers-Reydams collaborator, may well have been asked to complete La Fosse's landscapes when the cartoons arrived in Brussels.[31]

All four cartoons after La Fosse in the Gobelins *Metamorphoses* series (in addition to the three already discussed, there was also a *Bacchus Crowning Ariadne* re-

cently identified by Standen[32]) were painted by others, using pictures by La Fosse as models. The Leyniers-Reydams *Ovid's Fables* is the only documented case in which La Fosse personally worked with tapestries in mind. In fact, his lack of familiarity with the medium is evident. He forgot that Brussels low-warp weaving would reverse the composition. Thus, in *Apollo and Daphne* Cupid holds his bow in his right hand and a new arrow with his left (see fig. 1), and in *The Nymph and Apollo* the nymph presents her offering in her left hand (see fig. 11).

If it was unusual for La Fosse to work in this medium, it was even more uncommon for a Brussels workshop to commission cartoons from a French painter. French laws at this time discouraged the importation of rival Flemish tapestries. La Fosse, however, was internationally renowned as the greatest living colorist, translating into a contemporary idiom the

12. Gobelins Manufactory, Paris, after a painting by Charles de La Fosse, *Acis and Galatea,* from the *Metamorphoses* series, c. 1680, tapestry, 320 x 255 (126 x 100⅜) Rijksmuseum, Amsterdam

13. Gobelins Manufactory, Paris, after a painting by Charles de La Fosse, *Acis and Galatea,* from the *Metamorphoses* series, c. 1680, tapestry, 320 x 280 (126 x 110¼) Rijksmuseum, Amsterdam

lessons of Venetian Renaissance painting and Peter Paul Rubens. Urban Leyniers, for his part, was considered the finest master dyer in Brussels and, by implication, in Europe; his specialty was the dyeing of crimsons and flesh tones. Urban's father, Gaspar, also a renowned dyer, had been granted an official monopoly in Brussels after his crimsons were judged superior to French samples presumably from the Gobelins. In this period the comparison of Brussels tapestry with Parisian weavings was inevitable. Therefore, when Urban Leyniers and his brother Daniel II, primarily a weaver, entered into association with the important older weaver Henry II Reydams on 26 April 1712,[33] it was logical for the new enterprise to wish not only to show off its combined talents but also to match itself against contemporary Parisian creations. How better to begin than with a series by Charles de La Fosse? What better opportunity for the aging painter, restricted by mammoth religious commissions in France, to create one last large and prestigious secular cycle in which his gifts as a decorator could be deployed to the fullest?

As hoped, the first set of *Ovid's Fables* (which was, in fact, the second set of tapestries completed by the firm) had a brilliant success in Brussels in 1714, particularly because of the fine coloring.[34] Its union of French design with Brussels craftsmanship is also distinctive, as witnessed by past hesitations about the attribution of *Apollo and Daphne*. Ironically, of all La Fosse's large-scale secular wall decorations, only this somewhat atypical one, in the seemingly ephemeral medium of tapestry, has actually partially survived.

The Sources of La Fosse's *Apollo and Daphne*

With consummate grace, La Fosse's classic composition of *Diana's Return from the Hunt*, designed in the 1680s, explicitly

15. Atelier of Raphael or Sébastien François de la Planche, Paris, after an anonymous French design, *Apollo Pursuing Daphne*, from the *Story of Daphne* series, c. 1625–1675, tapestry, 342 x 441 (134⅛ x 173½) Museum of Fine Arts, Boston, Charles Potter Kling Fund

united the lessons of Titian and French academic narrative. To stress this union, several figures and their relative placement—especially in the Gobelins tapestry/Hermitage painting version of the composition—are derived directly from Titian's *Bacchanale of the Andrians* in the Prado,[35] and, as noted, La Fosse also carefully adhered to Ovid's text in good academic fashion. The inclusion of the composition in the Brussels tapestry cycle thus emphasized the painter's already internationally recognized control of his art. An apparently new design such as *Apollo and Daphne*, however, gave the aging master the opportunity to make a summarizing statement about mythological narrative in general.

La Fosse's choice of subject was not haphazard. The story of Apollo and Daphne is especially popular in Renaissance and baroque art, where it is found among Ovidian tales of the loves of the gods, in cycles about Apollo, and as a favorite metaphor for the power of love.[36] Though by 1544 it

already appears in tapestry as a subsidiary motif in Pieter Coecke van Aelst's *Triumph of Lust* from the *Seven Deadly Sins* series,[37] the flowering of independent hangings based on this subject did not begin until the seventeenth century. It is included in a Paris series entirely about Daphne, apparently woven in the la Planche atelier in the second quarter of the seventeenth century (fig. 15).[38] Another *Apollo and Daphne* woven in 1659–1660 at the Barberini manufactory in Rome is from an *Apollo* series.[39] The numerous later tapestries are generally in cycles of stories from Ovid's *Metamorphoses*; the Marillier archive illustrates eight different Flemish versions other than the La Fosse tapestry.[40]

There was also a successful French version in the Gobelins *Metamorphoses* series,[41] which was only one example of a particularly thriving fashion for the story of Apollo and Daphne in late seventeenth-century French art. The Sun King, Louis XIV, surrounded himself with flattering al-

16. Carlo Maratti, *Apollo and Daphne*, 1680–1681, oil on canvas, 221 x 224 (87 x 88) Musées Royaux des Beaux-Arts de Belgique, Brussels. ©A.C.L., Brussels

lusions to the sun god Apollo in poetry, ballet, and the decorations of his palaces. Apollo and Daphne was a favorite theme.[42] Louis XIV even commissioned a painting of *Apollo and Daphne* (fig. 16) from the Italian artist Carlo Maratti, who was considered by contemporary critics to be the artistic heir to the famed academic painting tradition of the Carracci family. The painting arrived in France in 1681.[43] It had such a poor reception at court that Maratti's great champion, the Italian biographer Giovan Pietro Bellori, wrote an apology in its defense, modeling his arguments on those used in the French painters' own Académie to praise such idols as Nicolas Poussin.[44]

The picture became, nonetheless, the most important example of Maratti's style in France and seems to have inspired a sort

of insiders' diversion, as French painters vied to surpass and correct its design. This may account, in part, for the proliferation of depictions of the story from 1681 on. Almost all of these include visual quotations from Maratti's figures and/or composition, so that artistically cultivated viewers would make the connection with the Italian painting and see how the French artist had improved upon it.[45] La Fosse's *Apollo and Daphne* is, in fact, one of the last in this long chain of compositions that, as it were, discuss the Maratti and its creative implications among one another.

Bellori's admiring analysis of Maratti's painting provides a good basis on which to judge how later French versions reacted to the canvas as well as the commentary itself. As Bellori writes, the picture is based on the story as told in Ovid's *Metamor-*

17. Gobelins Manufactory, Paris, after a design attributed to Louis II de Boulogne, *Apollo and Daphne*, from the *Metamorphoses* series, 1681–1730, tapestry
Present location unknown.
©Christie's, London

phoses.[46] After slaying the monstrous Python with his arrows, Apollo mocked Cupid, saying that he was too small to be a bowman. Cupid swore revenge and with an arrow struck Apollo with love for the nymph Daphne, daughter of the river god Peneus. Daphne, however, was an ardent follower of Diana, virgin goddess of the hunt, and, like her model, had taken a vow of chastity. She repulsed Apollo's advances and fled in fear. The sun god finally caught up with Daphne just as she saw the Peneus River and could appeal to her father, its deity, to destroy and transform her beauty. She was changed to a laurel plant literally under Apollo's impassioned embrace, and the disappointed god thereafter made the laurel his tree. He

is generally depicted wearing a crown of laurel leaves.

Maratti's painting shows the story's culmination, at the onset of Daphne's transformation. As Bellori explains, in this way the painter was able to unite several elements: Daphne's flight, Apollo overtaking her as she arrives at the Peneus River and appeals to her father for help, and the beginning of her metamorphosis. Peneus is actually represented as a river god reaching out as if to shield his daughter from Apollo. Another addition to Ovid's account is the figure of Cupid hovering above, gloating over his victory. Bellori writes that Maratti added Cupid to refer to his part in the story, and that he is flying off to tell his mother, Venus, goddess

18. Antoine Coypel, *Apollo and Daphne*, oil on canvas, 100 x 151 (39⅛ x 59½) Trianon de Marbre, Versailles

Beleori also writes that the painting shows how Maratti studied all the most important artistic sources, including antique sculpture, adding his own ideas and observations from nature to achieve a perfect beauty.[50] According to Bellori, Apollo follows the *Apollo Belvedere* in the Vatican, and Daphne derives from the *Venus of Cleomenes* in the Uffizi (now called the *Venus de' Medici*). Actually, only their torsos and physiognomies are somewhat comparable; the overall poses are quite different. As Ruda points out, however, Peneus recognizably derives from a back view of the *Torso Belvedere* in the Vatican.[51]

The Gobelins tapestry design, woven at least once by 1684, is one of the earliest datable French reactions to Maratti's painting. It may reflect a lost painting. Standen attributes the design to Louis II de Boulogne (fig. 17).[52] The reference to Maratti's painting is discernible in the poses of Apollo, Daphne, Peneus, and the naiad on the right with her back to the viewer. The French artist, however, strung out his figures across the composition to make a clearer line and eliminated the second river god, who confused the story. Moreover, this narrative follows Ovid to the letter; leaves now grow from Daphne's hair, and she is chastely dressed with only her thighs bared in flight, whereas Maratti had merely thrown fluttering drapery over parts of the nymph's anatomy instead of clothing her.[53] Cupid now appears in the distant sky.

A slightly later response to Maratti is Antoine Coypel's *Apollo and Daphne*, painted in 1689 for the Trianon (fig. 18).[54] There is some resemblance to the Italian painting in overall composition, but Coypel has emphasized a more classical pyramid layout. Maratti's single naiad on the right is replaced by two in the corner, whose vaguely similar poses have been modified so that they are more parallel to the picture plane. Peneus is now also at the right, his anguish evoked in a pose derived from a front view of the *Torso Belvedere*, in witty reply to Maratti. A naiad takes Peneus' original place in the foreground, stretching out her arms in imitation of the Italian model. Instead of a single Cupid, there are three erotes reveling in

of love, of his victory. Cupid appears in more or less this position in earlier representations, so the detail is not Maratti's invention.[47]

Though French academicians considered it bad style to combine episodes that took place at different times, Maratti's painting includes in the background two naiads and the river god Apidanus, one of the tributaries whom Ovid listed among the water deities commiserating with Peneus after the event.[48] Bellori turns the tables on the foreseen criticisms by lauding this addition precisely because of its adherence to the principles of academic unity. He says that it enhances Peneus' importance by evoking the great extent of his territories and that the figures thus enrich both the composition and the meaning.[49]

Bellori describes how each detail of Maratti's painting academically adheres to the poetic text and aptly illustrates the subject. In her haste, Daphne's beautiful limbs are revealed, as narrated by Ovid; her pose and expression evoke both fearful flight and stupefied transformation; roots grow from her feet and leaves from her hands; her flesh is befittingly pale. Apollo's complexion is ruddy because of the passion of his pursuit, and his draperies are of an appropriate, ardently flaming hue. Peneus has dark purple drapery and wet black hair, as suits a river god.

the scene. Daphne's pose remains similar to that in Maratti's painting, but her other foot is forward so that she more realistically has her back to Apollo. He is also similar to Maratti's figure, but the position of his legs is reversed and one arm is brought forward.[55] Like the designer of the Gobelins tapestry, Coypel combined these formal corrections with a careful revision of Maratti's narrative technique according to good academic practice: the second river god is again eliminated; leaves sprout from Daphne's hair, and she wears proper windblown clothing; Apollo, as Ovid described, is already hanging over Daphne's shoulders and has his arms partly around her as the transformation begins.

As already noted, Charles de La Fosse's tapestry design is also, in part, a reflection on Maratti's painting and Bellori's commentary. The work was a late addition to this pictorial debate, over thirty years after its inception. La Fosse, as is often the case with great painters, had developed in his old age an increasingly panoramic and at the same time critically economical eye. His design thus broadens the discussion to encompass the entire history of painting and tapestry since the Renaissance, and is consequently one of the culminations of Apollonian imagery under Louis XIV.[56] As will be shown, *Apollo and Daphne* also summarizes the stylistic tendencies of La Fosse's entire career, which explicitly paved the way to the enlightened century.

Reduced to the absolute narrative minimum—Apollo, Daphne, Peneus, Cupid, and a startled naiad—the design of La Fosse's *Apollo and Daphne* strictly adheres to academic unities of action. Its general composition refers back to early French tapestry tradition as well as to Maratti and his French critics. The similarly simplified la Planche tapestry, *Apollo Pursuing Daphne,* has analogously placed river deities, cascades, and tranquil distant bucolic figures, the latter underlining the drama with seventeenth-century irony (see fig. 15);[57] in fact the layouts of the two landscapes are nearly identical. However, La Fosse has retained the figure order of the later Gobelins design (see fig. 17). Since four La Fosse paintings had served as models for tapestries of the same

Gobelins series, the references to this design and to earlier tapestry tradition are all the more significant.[58] In these earlier tapestries, however, the protagonists move laterally across the composition, whereas in La Fosse's design they have been reorganized into a Coypel-like pyramid (fig. 18).[59]

Continuing to indicate by quotation the precursors on whom he was commenting, La Fosse followed Coypel once again in alluding to Maratti's Daphne, whose frontal pose is somewhat like that of Daphne in the tapestry. He also referred to the general pose of Maratti's Peneus, with his back to the viewer and arms held out, though Peneus' orientation seems to cite more directly the central nymph in Coypel's version. A drawing of this subject by Michel II Corneille, which still retains the figure composition of the Gobelins tapestry, shows Peneus in more or less the same pose as in the National Gallery of Art's tapestry (fig. 19). Daphne's pose is also closer to La Fosse's. This drawing seems to represent another intermediate phase in the French dialogue.[60]

The decisive inspiration for the position of La Fosse's Daphne appears to have come, however, from Titian's *Perseus and Andromeda*, then in Paris (fig. 20).[61] Moreover, La Fosse's Apollo is an even more unexpected and pointed commentary on the academic debate. The figure does not derive from any ancient sculpture or recent version of the theme. Rather, as in the la Planche tapestry, it cites Jacopo Caraglio's print of *Apollo and Daphne*, engraved after a drawing by Perino del Vaga (fig. 21).[62] The reference to the sixteenth-century print is emphasized by depicting Apollo's bow on the ground and by imitating the design of his quiver in Caraglio's version. Daphne and Apollo thus broaden the discussion to include Titian and the Italian Renaissance as important sources for La Fosse and, it is implied, for mythological painting in general.[63]

Like his French predecessors in the Maratti debate, La Fosse has also academically reread Ovid. Apollo is literally about to touch Daphne (but he is not as close as in Coypel's version), and she is again clothed, with her limbs bared in flight, though no leaves sprout from her hair. All earlier expository devices have also been enhanced both in terms of clarity and naturalism. Daphne now more explicitly unites the phases of the action. Even as, with her left leg still raised in flight, she cries out and repels Apollo with her left arm, her right fingers sprout foliage, and her forward foot literally becomes rooted in the earth, engendering leaves. Daphne's expression betrays speechless stupor at her transformation, but her eyes still retain their fear of Apollo. La Fosse also stressed the figures' different complexions as Bellori points out that Maratti had (the nymph white with fright, Peneus dark-skinned, Daphne pale, and Apollo with the ruddy cheeks of impassioned exertion). As in Maratti's painting, the colors of the clothing are also appropriate thematically (Apollo's ardent red cloak, Peneus' watery blue drapery).

Compared with all the seventeenth-century sources that La Fosse's narrative cites and therefore implies that it equals or "surpasses" on their own ground, there is one essential difference in approach evident in the tapestry. Ovid says Daphne prayed for her beauty to be destroyed, but La Fosse took care not to violate the grace of the female form as had Maratti and his commentators in their effort to follow the text so literally. The leaves sprout from the ends of Daphne's fingers without distorting them, and her rooted foot remains shapely without being disfigured by bark and roots. Her flesh is still soft and feminine in color and texture. In this concern for female beauty La Fosse has again followed the example of Titian. However, his overall method even more closely parallels that of Peter Paul Rubens, who based his carefully measured compositions on Titian and other Renaissance prototypes but reworked them with baroque sensuality. Even the pastel head studies used to work up the designs for the tapestry (see figs. 4 and 6) are a study technique derived from Rubens. La Fosse adapted this technique to his own working methods late in his career, when he returned to the study of the works of the Antwerp painter. This renewed meditation on Rubens brought La Fosse's style to the final synthesis with which it ushered in the eighteenth century.[64] In fact, one might say that Charles de La Fosse's tapestry, *Apollo and Daphne,* despite its careful crafting, emphatically declares an end to rigid seventeenth-century academic tradition and the beginning of a new era, in which idealized femininity was to reign.

Thus, at the close of a long, distinguished career, La Fosse evoked in *Apollo and Daphne* the sources he saw as antecedents for his own final word on the theme and for his late stylistic credo in general. They document his fascination with Titian and the Italian Renaissance rather than Roman antiquity, his dedication to his French academic roots, despite his *Rubéniste-coloriste* tendencies, and his observation of the debate around Maratti's canvas within the artistic entourage of the Sun King. The tapestry's masterful union of these contradictory tendencies of painterly style and Venetian coloring with utter academic refinement, as well as with Rubens' Italian Renaissance-derived conciseness and exaltation of the female form, is an optimal illustration of why Charles de La Fosse was among the great progenitors of eighteenth-century French art.

NOTES

1. Acc. no. 1951.1.1; see Candace Adelson in *Western Decorative Arts Part II, The Collections of the National Gallery of Art Systematic Catalogue* (Washington, forthcoming). Among the colleagues who have aided my research, to all of whom I am most grateful, special thanks go to: Gérard Auguier, Henriette and Philippe Baby, Mary Ballard Jenkins, Ariane de Courcel, Ingrid De Meûter, Guy Delmarcel, Wendy Hefford, Pierre Rosenberg, Jeffrey Ruda, Antoine Schnapper, Edith Appleton Standen, and Isabelle Van Tichelen.

2. H. C. Marillier, *Subject Catalogue of Tapestries*, manuscript, 50 vols., Victoria and Albert Museum, Department of Textiles, inv. T37–1946, T37R: s.v. "Apollo," 19; and *Mythologies-various*: 31. I would like to thank former head keeper Santina Levey, Wendy Hefford, and all the textile and costume staff of the Victoria and Albert Museum for having made this resource abundantly available during my research despite the department's heavy schedule.

3. Documents in the National Gallery of Art, Washington, curatorial files; see also Adelson, in Washington, forthcoming, note 1.

4. Adelson, in Washington, forthcoming; see also note 1.

5. Emile Jellinek-Mercedes sale, American Art Association, New York, 20 February 1926, lot 8, repro., as "Paris, seventeenth century"; Marillier *Subject Catalogue*, T37R: s.v. "Apollo," 18, repro. This is probably the same piece previously bought by Duveen from the Mellier sale, Christie's, London, 14 June 1901, lot 25, as "old French"; Marillier *Subject Catalogue*, T37R: s.v. "Apollo," 25.

6. On the *bastons rompus* border, see Edith A. Standen, "Some Beauvais Tapestries Related to Bérain," in *Acts of the Tapestry Symposium November 1976* (San Francisco, 1979), 212, 218 notes 15–16.

7. De Meûter, personal communication, 1985. The signed set of *Famous Men* was auctioned at Sotheby's, London, 18 July 1980, lots 106–109, repro.; according to notes in the tapestry photo archives, Musées Royaux d'art et d'histoire, Brussels, *Aristides* (lot 107 in the 1980 sale) was reauctioned by Sotheby's in London, 10 April 1981, and in Monte Carlo, 23 February 1986, lot 813; *Alcibiades* (in two pieces, lot 109 in the 1980 sale) was at the Vigo Sternberg gallery, London, in 1984.

8. Ad Reydams, "Les Reydams tapissiers bruxellois," *Annales de la Société royale d'archéologie de Bruxelles* 22 (1908), 104–105, 115, nos. 2, 4, 29; Marillier *Subject Catalogue*, *Mythologies-various*: 31; Heinrich Göbel, *Wandteppiche*, 3 parts in 6 vols. (Leipzig, 1923–1934), I, 1:342.

9. Ingrid De Meûter plans a new study of the manuscript, which records these tapestries, first published by Reydams 1908, but see also Göbel 1923–1934, I, 1:341–348; Marthe Crick-Kuntziger, "The Tapestries in the Palace of Liège," *Burlington Magazine* 50 (1927), 177 note 4; and Marthe Crick-Kuntziger, "De

quelques tapisseries bruxelloises des XVIᵉ et XVIIᵉ siècles," *Bulletin des Musées royaux d'art et d'histoire* 25 (1953), 13–23.

10. Nationalmuseum, Stockholm, inv. NM 2846/1863; Per Bjurström, *French Drawings Sixteenth and Seventeenth Centuries*, vol. 2 of *Drawings in Swedish Public Collections* (Stockholm, 1976), no. 455, repro.

11. Louvre, inv. 27433; Jean Guiffrey and Pierre Marcel, *Inventaire général des dessins du Musée du Louvre et du Musée de Versailles. Ecole française* (Paris, 1907), 7:68–69, no. 5459, repro.

12. For instance, *The Rape of Dejanira* and *Galatea*, Musée des Beaux-Arts, Agen; the *Triumph of Bacchus*, Louvre; and *Hercules between Virtue and Vice*, Musée des Beaux-Arts, Nevers; Margret Stuffmann, "Charles de La Fosse et sa position dans la peinture française à la fin du XVIIᵉ siècle," *Gazette des Beaux-Arts* 64 (July–August 1964), 108–109 respectively nos. 52, 53bis, 54, 55. La Fosse's only wall decoration comparable in format to tapestry of which visual record survives is his Montagu House *Diana and Actaeon* (known from a watercolor by George Scharf, 1845; Stuffmann 1964, 78 fig. 39). The figures are also in an extensive landscape (probably by Jacques Rousseau).

13. The small, stylistically late Orléans painting may even postdate the tapestry design, as it seems to show a further evolution in the treatment of the subject; Mary O'Neill, *Musée des Beaux-Arts d'Orléans, Catalogue critique. Les Peintures de l'école française des XVIᵉ et XVIIᵉ siècles*, 2 vols. (Nantes, 1981), 1:84, no. 90, inv. 541; 2:83 repro. O'Neill also noted a La Fosse *Apollo and Daphne* listed in a 1703 inventory. Two other paintings of *Apollo and Daphne* in the Musée Magnin, Dijon, have been associated with La Fosse. Stuffmann 1964, 114 no. X, rejects one. The second is known also in a version at Sans-Souci, Potsdam; Wolfgang Stechow, *Apollo und Dafne*, vol. 23 of *Studien der Bibliothek Warburg* (Leipzig and Berlin, 1932), fig. 38 (Potsdam); Stuffmann 1964, 99 no. 10 (Dijon). Antoine Schnapper, "Louis de Silvestre: tableaux de jeunesse," *Revue du Louvre* 23, 1 (1973), 23 fig. 7 (Potsdam), demonstrates that it is by Louis de Silvestre (engraved in 1707), influenced by La Fosse. For the Versailles Apollo, painted c. 1672–1681, see Stuffmann 1964, 71 fig. 34, 72, 100 no. 17.

14. Reydams 1908, 104 no. 2, 105 no. 4, 115 no. 29. Though other undocumented sets may have been woven, the manuscript seems to give a detailed description of the firm's production. After Henry Reydams' death in 1719, the shop was run by the two Leyniers brothers until Daniel II's death in 1728, after which Urban and his son Daniel III ran it until 1745; letter from Ingrid De Meûter, 13 June 1988. Daniel III then maintained the shop alone until 1767. The two early sets of *Ovid's Fables*, and hence the National Gallery of Art's tapestry, were therefore made during the first period, under the Leyniers-Reydams association. The similar borders of the

signed Leyniers-Reydams *Famous Men* further confirm this hypothesis as to dating.

15. Edith A. Standen, "Ovid's *Metamorphoses*: A Gobelins Tapestry Series," *Metropolitan Museum Journal* 23 (1988), 158–162, 189 notes 42–47, discusses the variants of the composition.

16. The present location of the first is unknown; sold at Galerie Charpentier, Paris, 6 April 1960, lot 139, repro.; and at Nouveau Drouot, Paris, 19 March 1982 (Ader, rooms 5 and 6), lot 99, color repro., as noted by Edith A. Standen, *European Post-Medieval Tapestries and Related Hangings in The Metropolitan Museum of Art*, 2 vols. (New York, 1985), 1:319; and Standen 1988, 189 note 47. The second example is presently with Luciano Coen, Rome (300 x 530 cm). For the Toronto picture, which is in mirror image to the tapestry, see *Paintings and Sculpture. Illustrations of Selected Paintings and Sculpture from the Collection, The Art Gallery of Toronto* (Toronto, 1959), 22, inv. 55/9, repro.; Stuffmann 1964, 104 no. 34, repro. The figures are exactly those of the tapestry's center, with similar dogs behind the kneeling nymph, a detail not found in other versions. However, the reclining nymph below Diana is missing.

17. E. J. Kalf, "Drie Leyniers-tapijten te Middelburg," *Artes Textiles* 5 (1959–1960), 112–113; Ovid, *Metamorphoses* 3.168, Loeb Classical Library, Latin authors, trans. Frank Justus Miller (Cambridge, Mass., and London, 1939–1944).

18. Ovid, *Metamorphoses* 3.158–160.

19. There is always the possibility that these tapestries are from a fourth, undocumented *Ovid's Fables* set woven when Urban ran the workshop beginning in 1728.

20. Sold at Christie's, London, 19 May 1931, lot 145, as noted by Standen 1988, 189 note 47.

21. In the description of Peter Van der Borght's six *Triumphs of the Gods*, the composition is identifiable because of the detail of the nymph removing Diana's sandals; J. Denucé, *Antwerp Art Tapestry and Trade*, vol. 4 of *Historical Sources for the Study of Flemish Art* (Antwerp, 1936), doc. no. 34, 396; Kalf 1959–1960, 112 note 22. Both Frans and Peter Van der Borght were active in the period after the last documented weaving of *Ovid's Fables* by the Leyniers (1721); see Alphonse Wauters, *Les tapisseries bruxelloises* (Brussels, 1878, and reprint 1973), 370–374; Göbel 1923–1934, I, 1:299–403. In 1757 Daniel III Leyniers and Peter Van der Borght collaborated on a series of *Scenes from Military Life* designed by Hyacinth de la Pegna; there was thus exchange between the two families; Göbel 1923–1934, I, 1:352–353, 403; I, 2: fig. 298.

22. Presently with Luciano Coen, Rome, *Apollo* 130, 331 (September 1989), 36 color repro.

23. It is executed in chalk on blue paper and is in a private collection. This drawing was recognized and kindly pointed out by Pierre Rosenberg in a personal communication.

24. Bjurström 1976, no. 459, repro.

25. Christie's, London, 28 June 1934, lot 118; property of Captain S. H. Christy, bought by Koffe. Marillier, *Subject Catalogue*, T37R:24 (partial photograph). The heads of the central woman and Apollo recall in pose two others of the La Fosse pastels in the Nationalmuseum, Stockholm, though the photograph of the tapestry is not clear enough to make this connection certain. Compare Apollo with inv. NM 2845/1863; Bjurström 1976, no. 454; the pastel is in the same direction as the tapestry, and the model seems to have been a young woman (Apollo is effeminate in the tapestry). Compare the woman with inv. NM 2847/1863, Bjurström 1976, no. 457, reversed in respect to the tapestry.

26. Ovid, *Metamorphoses* 2.68–69.

27. La Fosse's painting is *in situ*; Antoine Schnapper, *Tableaux pour le Trianon de marbre 1688–1714* (Paris and The Hague, 1967), 78 no. 1, 11, fig. 10; the composition is quite different from that of the tapestry, though Tethys' gestures are somewhat similar to the nymph's. On the theme, see Jennifer Montagu, "Oeuvres de Charles Le Brun," *La donation Baderou au Musée de Rouen. Ecole française*, vol. 1 of *Etudes de la Revue du Louvre* (Paris, 1980), 42–43 (thanks to Jeffrey Ruda for this reference). Montagu explains that it evolved through a linguistically induced conflation of the aged sea goddess Tethys with the beautiful nymph Thetis, mother of Achilles. The most popular scenes were apparently Apollo greeting Tethys in the evening after his daily journey and Apollo taking leave of her in the morning—thus at sunset and sunrise. If La Fosse's tapestry does indeed illustrate this subject, it is perhaps unique in representing a moment between the two and may have been intended to refer to (France's?) maritime or mercantile power and wealth.

28. Standen 1988, 150–155 figs. 1–4, gives the history of the Gobelins tapestries and lists the La Fosse paintings; Stuffmann 1964, 108–109 no. 53. On the series, see also Maurice Fenaille, *Etat général des tapisseries de la Manufacture des Gobelins*, 6 vols. (Paris, 1903–1923), 3:121–132.

29. La Fosse's *Rape of Europa* was painted in England for the duke of Montagu; Stuffmann 1964, 105 no. 38a repro. A La Fosse drawing of the subject was noted by Alfred Darcel, "Troyes et ses expositions d'art," *Gazette des Beaux-Arts* 17 (1864), 341.

30. Standen 1988, 189 note 47, before the series' reconstruction, had suggested a print source for the *Diana* cartoon. The flamelike fragmentation of light and color and the multiplication of facets in the drapery in *Apollo and Daphne* are typical of La Fosse's late style. It is interesting to compare the similar finish of the figures in the Leyniers-Reydams *Diana* with the more classical treatment in the Gobelins version of the same composition, copied by collaborators of the manufactory from a much earlier and hence less luminescent painting by the artist (perhaps similar in execution to the Toronto canvas, fig. 9). In 1732, well after La Fosse's death, two more tapestries on cartoons by "La Fosse" appear in the Leyniers-Reydams records: a *Virgin* copied after Jean-

Baptiste Santerre, and *Jesus Healing the Leper* after Rubens (Reydams 1908, 126 no. 59; Göbel 1923–1934, I, 1:348). It has been assumed that these were by Charles de La Fosse, but it seems odd that he should copy a younger contemporary such as Santerre. The cartoons were probably by a little-known homonym.

31. On La Fosse's collaboration with landscape painters, see note 12. For *Neptune* (present location unknown), see Göbel 1923–1934, I, 2: fig. 292.

32. Standen 1988, 154–157, figs. 5 and 6.

33. Reydams was a relative, having married their cousin Jeanne-Catherine Leyniers in 1675. On the history of the families and the joint workshop, see Wauters 1884; Reydams 1908; Göbel 1923–1934, I, 1: 341–348, 351–352; I, 2: figs. 289–293, 302; Crick-Kuntziger 1927, 172–183; Heinrich Göbel, in Thieme-Becker 23:173 s.v. "Leyniers"; anonymous, in Thieme-Becker 28:211 s.v. "Reydams"; H. C. Marillier, *Handbook to the Teniers Tapestries* (London, 1932); Marthe Crick-Kuntziger, *De tapijtwerken in het Stadhuis te Brussel* (Antwerp and Utrecht, 1944), 41–44; Crick-Kuntziger 1953; Ingrid De Meûter, "De wandtapijtkunst in de zuidelijke Nederlanden," in *België in de 18de eeuw, Kritische bibliografie; La Belgique au 18ᵉ siècle, bibliographie critique* (Brussels, 1983), 364–382; Adelson, in Washington, forthcoming, see note 1. Though Reydams and Göbel maintain that the partnership was continued by Henry Reydams' wife until her death in 1733, Crick-Kuntziger (1927, 177) and Ingrid De Meûter (see also note 14) maintain on the basis of documents that after Henry Reydams' death in 1719, the shop was run by the Leyniers family alone. It is possible, nonetheless, that Jeanne-Catherine Leyniers maintained a financial interest in the concern. The problem bears further study.

34. The firm's first set, completed in 1713, was of the *Famous Men after Plutarch*. According to the documents, the duchess of Arenberg was so pleased with her *Ovid's Fables* "qu'elle la fit examiner par toutes les connaissances, tant peintres que tapissiers, et on reconnut qu'elle [the set] était travaillée dans la dernière perfection et finesse et qu'il n'y avait jusqu' à présent jamais plus à tendre à la perfection de la dite tenture par l'ordre que l'on y trouvait dans la direction des couleurs"; Reydams 1908, 104. It is curious that two of the three documented sets of *Ovid's Fables*, including the *editio princeps*, were ordered by women. La Fosse's flattering approach to his female models must have appealed to these probably rather spirited widows. If the dowager duchess of Arenberg was in the market for an appropriately feminine set, this might have been a factor prompting the Leyniers-Reydams concern to approach La Fosse for the cartoons in the first place. On the other hand, the series included only subjects favored in French court art. In particular, *Apollo and Tethys* (if that is indeed the theme of *The Nymph and Apollo*) was a subject uniquely favored by Louis XIV, and, as will be demonstrated, La Fosse's *Apollo and Daphne* was designed in reply to a French academic painting debate. This may indicate some speculation by the

Leyniers-Reydams firm that, using La Fosse's name as a draw, they would subsequently be able to export sets even to France. This prospect would have been thwarted by the death of Louis XIV in 1715, and with it the fading of his imagery.

35. Harold E. Wethey, *The Paintings of Titian*, 3 vols. (London, 1969–1975), 3:152–153 cat. no. 15, pl. 57. The sleeping nymph in the lower left corner of the tapestry is a direct quotation from the nymph at the lower right of the painting; the nymph with the dog in the tapestry probably is derived from the dancing woman to the right of Titian's painting; the nymph pouring liquid (perfume?) over Diana's hair from a flask echoes the man pouring wine at the left of the *Bacchanale*. Titian's painting was a favorite source of Nicolas Poussin's, who studied it in the Ludovisi Collection in Rome at the same time that he made the careful studies from Titian's *Worship of Venus* noted at length by Giovan Pietro Bellori, *Le vite de' pittori scultori et architetti moderni* (Rome, 1672), 494–495; see Candace Adelson, "Nicolas Poussin et les tableaux du Studiolo d'Isabelle d'Este," *Revue du Louvre* 4 (1975), 240. The *Bacchanale of the Andrians* was thus known to all seventeenth-century French academic painters, who idolized Poussin. Stuffmann 1964, 104 no. 34, suggests that La Fosse's central group derives from Domenichino's *Rinaldo and Armida* in the Louvre; Richard E. Spear, *Domenichino*, 2 vols. (New Haven and London, 1982), 1:221 cat. no. 68; 2: pl. 234. The layout of the figure composition, which works diagonally across the painting, is similar, and there is a vague resemblance in the poses, but the nymph with the flask is closer in pose to Titian.

36. Stechow 1932; A. Pigler, *Barockthemen*, 2 vols. (Budapest, 1974), 2:27–29.

37. Rotraud Bauer and Jan Karel Steppe, *Tapisserien der Renaissance nach Entwürfen von Pieter Coecke van Aelst* [exh. cat., Schloss Halbturn] (Vienna, 1981), fig. 9.

38. Adolph S. Cavallo, "The Splendour Falls on Castle Walls," *Bulletin, Museum of Fine Arts, Boston* 60, no. 321 (1962), 63, 70–82; Adolph S. Cavallo, *Tapestries of Europe and of Colonial Peru in the Museum of Fine Arts, Boston*, 2 vols. (Boston, 1967), 1:129–134 nos. 37–38; 2: pls. 37–38; Candace Adelson, *European Tapestries in the Minneapolis Institute of Arts* (Minneapolis, forthcoming).

39. Göbel 1923–1934, 2, 1:420; 2, 2: fig. 435; Anna Maria De Strobel, *Le arazzerie romane dal XVII al XIX secolo* (Rome, 1989), 41–42; Adelson, Minneapolis, forthcoming, note 38.

40. Marillier *Subject Catalogue* T37R:16–19; T37V:88, 91, 103; *Mythologies*: 33, 38.

41. For the Gobelins *Metamorphoses* piece, see below and note 52.

42. On Apollo and Daphne imagery during Louis XIV's early reign, see Jean-Pierre Néraudau, *L'Olympe du Roi-Soleil* (Paris, 1986), 46, 51, 100, 129–130, 158–160, 187, 220.

43. Now in the Musées Royaux des beaux-arts, Brussels, inv. 269; *Musées royaux des beaux-arts de Belgique. Département d'Art Ancien. Catalogue inventaire de la peinture ancienne* (Brussels, 1984), 183, repro.

44. "Dafne trasformata in lauro pittura del signor Carlo Maratti dedicata a' trionfi di Luigi XIV il magno descritta in una lettera ad un cavaliere forestiero," in Giovan Pietro Bellori, *Le vite dei pittori, scultori ed architetti moderni,* 3 vols. (Pisa, 1821), 3:239–256 (first published in 1731, but written for a correspondent in France before Bellori's death in 1696, probably c. 1681–1682). The literary model was Le Brun's 1667 lesson on Poussin's *Gathering of Manna;* André Félibien, *Entretiens sur les vies et sur les ouvrages des plus excellens peintres,* 6 vols. (Trevous, 1725), 5:402–428. Le Brun's discourse was a model of academic analysis for contemporaries; see Rensselaer W. Lee, "Ut Pictura Poesis. The Humanistic Theory of Painting," *Art Bulletin* 22 (1940), 223–224. See also Stechow 1932, 34, 38–39, 61–63 fig. 46.

45. Stechow 1932, 38–39, notes the relation of these compositions to Maratti's design, and Schnapper 1967, 64, discusses the Italian painting's influence and Maratti's relation to French painting. For other French examples of the theme, see Standen 1988, 183 figs. 48–50. There are also drawings by François Le Moine (Musée de Grenoble) and by Noël Nicholas Coypel (Museum der bildenden Künste, Leipzig) called *Apollo and the Serpent Python.*

46. Ovid, *Metamorphoses* 1.452–567.

47. A tendency to add Cupid to the scene is already evident in the sixteenth century; see, for example, the illustrated 1557 Lyons edition of the *Metamorphoses;* Svetlana Alpers, *The Decoration of the Torre de la Parada,* vol. 9 of the *Corpus Rubenianum Ludwig Burchard* (London and New York, 1971), fig. 53.

48. Ovid, *Metamorphoses* 1.568–582.

49. Bellori 1821, 3:251–252.

50. Bellori 1821, 3:254.

51. Jeffrey Ruda, personal communication, 1989.

52. The piece illustrated was sold at Christie's, London, 2 December 1971, lot 152. Another example is in the Schloss at Bayreuth; Standen 1988, 182–184 fig. 47. Others are known from auctions; Standen 1988, 191 notes 84, 89. In 1684 a piece was apparently inventoried in Louis XIV's collection; Fenaille 1903–1923, 3:121.

53. See Ovid's quite visual description, *Metamorphoses* 1.527–530, 540–552:

The winds bared her limbs, the opposing breezes set her garments a-flutter as she ran, and a light air flung her locks streaming behind her. Her beauty was enhanced by flight. . . . But he ran the more swiftly, borne on the wings of love, gave her no time to rest, hung over her fleeing shoulders and breathed on the hair that streamed over her neck. Now was her strength all gone, and pale with fear and utterly overcome by the toil of her swift flight, seeing her father's waters near, she cried: "O father, help! If your waters hold divinity; change and destroy this beauty by which I pleased o'er well." Scarce had she thus prayed when a down-dragging numbness seized her limbs, and her soft sides were begirt with thin bark. Her hair was changed to leaves, her arms to branches. Her feet, but now so swift, grew fast in sluggish roots, and her head was now but a tree's top. Her gleaming beauty alone remained.

54. Recently replaced in the Trianon de Marbre at Versailles; MV 8375; Nicole Garnier, *Antoine Coypel 1661–1722* (Paris, 1989), 104–105, no. 32, col. pl. IV. Copied in a print by Nicolas Tardieu; Schnapper 1967, 28 fig. 23, 84 no. 1.

55. Schnapper 1967, 63, notes that Coypel's Daphne cites Maratti's to indicate that a comparison between the two paintings is intended. Coypel may also have generally derived his composition from Poussin's *Pan and Syrinx,* Staatliche Kunstsammlungen, Dresden; Anthony Blunt, *Nicolas Poussin,* 2 vols. (New York, 1967), 2: fig. 107b.

56. Louis XIV died, it should be recalled, only a short time later in 1715.

57. Museum of Fine Arts, Boston, acc. no. 62.330; Cavallo 1967, 1:129–134 no. 38; 2: pl. 38.

58. The Gobelins tapestry's linear layout also seems to derive ultimately from the earlier pre–Gobelins tapestry or a common source.

59. Coypel and La Fosse both utilized Cupid to create a diagonal in space, continuing one side of the pyramid, but without returning to Maratti's cluttered oblique "X" composition.

60. Louvre, inv. F.7 25455; Guiffrey-Marcel 1907, 3:80–81 no. 2326, repro.

61. Now in the Wallace Collection, London; Wethey 1969–1975, 3:169–172 no. 30, pls. 134–136. Titian's Andromeda, if one reverses the position of the legs, is actually far closer than Maratti's Daphne to the basic stance and proportions of the Aphrodite of Cnidos type, of which the *Venus de' Medici* is one example. La Fosse's Daphne retains those parts of Andromeda's pose derived from the ancient statue—the twisted head and (more or less) the position of the legs. La Fosse's choice of model is thus possibly also a veiled comment on how to cite ancient sculpture, and on who knew how to do it to perfection. Titian was a master at converting ancient statues into sensuous flesh.

62. Bartsch, 18.

63. The Perino-Caraglio composition ultimately also inspired Daphne's planar pose and the positioning of Apollo in the tapestry. La Fosse may actually have thought he was again referring to Titian here. The *Apollo and Daphne* from the destroyed paintings of the gods once at Blenheim Castle follows Caraglio's composition exactly, except for the bow and Peneus' right arm. It was considered to be by Titian, and engraved with that attribution by Pieter Stevens van Gunst, as well as in 1709 by John Smith. Stechow

1932, fig. 32, tentatively attributes the painting to Padovanino. When he was in England, La Fosse may have seen the original painting and taken an interest in Caraglio's print in the belief that it, too, had been designed by his Venetian idol.

64. The technique was in turn adapted by Watteau. On La Fosse's similar studies for his *Adoration of the Magi* for Notre-Dame (1711–1715) and their relation to Rubens and Watteau, see Jean-Pierre Cuzin, "Deux dessins du British Museum: Watteau, ou plutôt La Fosse," *Revue du Louvre* 31, 1 (1981), 19–21. Cuzin states that there were eight such La Fosse heads in the 1741 Crozat sale.

ISABELLE VAN TICHELEN AND GUY DELMARCEL

Marks and Signatures on Ancient Flemish Tapestries

A Methodological Contribution

The obligatory and systematic interweaving of marks on Flemish tapestries originated in an edict published by the Brussels town magistrate on 16 May 1528. In order to control production and protect against falsification, this edict obliged local weavers or their contractors to weave the city mark and their personal mark on pieces larger than six ells.[1] The interweaving of the Brussels mark was actually a new way of applying a seal to the tapestries. Beginning 7 April 1450, prior to the sale of tapestries, Brussels weavers were required to submit them for inspection of materials. The seal of the weavers' guild was attached to the approved pieces as a quality label.[2] This label was probably a seal made of wax or lead, which was fastened to the weaving with a cord.[3] From 1513, as a measure against falsification, tapestries made in Enghien (Dutch: Edingen) were provided with a lead seal composed of the town coat of arms and the letter *E*.[4] We do not know the composition of the seal of the Brussels weavers' guild, but it was probably identical to an almost illegible seal preserved on a document of 7 May 1562.[5]

Until 1472, seals were applied to the Brussels tapestries in the Chapel of Saint Christophorus "int Ruysbroec," where the seal of the guild was kept.[6] Beginning in 1475, the inspectors of the tapestry guild were required to visit the workshops at least

three times a year in order to check the materials.[7] Because these controls were not actually maintained and abuses occurred daily, the edict of 1528 was promulgated, obliging Brussels weavers and contractors of tapestry work to interweave tapestry marks in accordance with the local technique of weaving on low-warp looms. They were ordered to place their own weavers' mark "on one side" of the piece and "on the other side" the Brussels city mark—a red shield flanked on either side by the letter *B* (Brabant-Brussels) (fig. 1).[8] Contraventions were to be punished by imposing a set fine on weavers who failed to mark their pieces and the confiscation of tapestries woven outside Brussels but interwoven with the Brussels city mark.[9]

In order to detect any abuse, the weavers' marks were registered in a special book by the guild. This register was destroyed in the Guildhall fire of 1690.[10] The loss of this valuable source for the identification of Brussels tapestries is only partly offset by a small number of archives in which monograms of weavers are identified.[11]

The Brussels practice of weaving the mark of the city and that of the weaver in the borders was imitated shortly thereafter in Enghien. Seals were already being used in Enghien, as mentioned above, and this was simply a new way of marking, probably introduced before 1535.[12]

It soon became obvious that the marks

fig. 2

woven on tapestries could not fully guarantee the authenticity and quality of the work. About 1540, several abuses of "painting up" tapestries were noted in the southern Netherlands. Weavers from Brussels and Enghien were also involved in these practices.[13] As the tapestry industry was "one of the most famous and principal trades and businesses of the country," Charles v promulgated a general edict on 16 May 1544. According to article 41, every weaver, whether residing in a tapestry center or "outside the towns of Leuven, Brussels, Antwerp, Bruges, Oudenaarde, Aalst, Enghien, Binche, Ath, Lille, Tournai, and other free places" had to interweave in the tapestry border his own mark next to the sign "ordered by the city."[14] This made it possible not only to determine the origin of each piece but also to detect frauds in quality or origin.[15] Falsification of marks resulted in corporal punishment and exclusion from the guild.[16]

Oudenaarde was apparently the first town to comply with the emperor's request to interweave the mark of the city and weaver. On 15 January 1545 the local authorities determined the form of the city mark for their tapestry industry: a pair of spectacles "breaking behind a yellow field with three red bends."[17] Special care was taken over the finished products in accordance with article 67 of the general edict.[18] A resolution of 16 January 1671 prohibited the weavers from wrapping their tapestries before the arrival of guild inspectors.[19] This measure was intended to eliminate the falsification of marks, an example of which is mentioned in a document of 1640.[20]

As indicated by the 1671 resolution, the tapestries of Oudenaarde were still inspected at the workshop or the weaver's shop at the end of the seventeenth century, as stipulated by the general edict of 1544. This was not the case in Brussels, where the edict was not published until 26 October 1546.[21] It may be assumed that the imposed inspection initially took place in the workshop or weaver's shop. However, at the beginning of the seventeenth century tapestry sealers were apparently available to check finished tapestries three times a week in the room of

1. Brussels city mark, *Isaac Blessing Jacob*, c. 1534, tapestry
Royal Museums of Art and History, Brussels, inv. no. 8584. Photo A.C.L. Brussels

the corporation of the city. From 15 March 1657, after the opening of the Brussels "Tapestry Hall," the weavers of the town had to bring their tapestries there for control or the application of a seal.[22] It is not clear if this refers to an extra inspection for all tapestries on sale, or if the inspections at the weavers' workshops had been abolished to eliminate abuses.

Bruges was probably the first place, after the capital of Brabant, to publish the imperial ordinance, on 5 January 1547.[23] The weavers of Bruges, like their colleagues from Oudenaarde, had previously never used any identification mark or seal. Some months after the publication of the edict, the municipality of Bruges conferred on the local weavers' guild the crowned Gothic *B* as city mark. Already used for official purposes since the beginning of the fourteenth century (e.g., the city seals), this mark was replaced at the end of the sixteenth century by another, the so-called *broche*, the bobbin of the high-warp loom (fig. 2).[24] In contrast with the city mark, the marks of the Bruges workshops do not appear frequently on tapestries, perhaps indicating that the weaving of their mark was not compulsory in this city.

Some cities in the southern Netherlands did not agree to certain articles of the imperial edict of 1544 and therefore initially refused its publication. Ghent, for instance, delayed publication until 1553.[25] No tap-

estry with the city mark of Ghent is known, nor does the register with the marks of the weavers of this town still exist.[26] The marks of some tapestry weavers have been found, but only in documents.[27] Antwerp also postponed the edict year after year, claiming that this law curtailed freedom of trade.[28] Marks on Antwerp tapestries were removed in this town and replaced by the Brussels city mark, which led the weavers' guild of Brussels to lodge a complaint at the Council of Brabant in Antwerp in 1560.[29] The ordinance was finally published in Antwerp on 28 July 1562, but documents imposing a defined city mark on the weavers have not been found.[30] Marks on existing tapestries show that several types have been used: a stylized reproduction of the Antwerp castle with a hand on either

side; a mark clearly inspired by the coat of arms of the county of Antwerp; a hand followed by a letter *A*; and an adapted form of the Brussels city mark, namely the initials *B-A*, standing for Brabant-Antwerp (fig. 3).[31]

The publication of the general edict did not put an end to misuse of the Brussels city mark. The oldest known case of imposture dates from 1559, when the tapestry merchant Nicolaas Hellinck of Enghien was accused of obscuring the Enghien marks with ink and selling the tapestries as those of Brussels.[32] Brussels tapestries were famous for their aesthetic and material qualities and therefore more expensive. On 17 August 1617, in response to the demand of the Brussels weavers, King Philip III of Spain promulgated a new ordinance.[33] It attempted to prevent the placement of Brussels marks on weavings from other locales, an abuse that was very damaging to the Brussels tapestry industry. The use of the letter *B* and the red shield was then prohibited on pieces not woven in Brussels. Moreover, all pieces of the same tapestry series had to be woven in the same town.

The Antwerp weavers immediately appealed this edict.[34] Objecting to being dominated by their Brussels colleagues, they argued that "the prohibition of the letter *B* in a weavers' mark would falsify several marks of Antwerp weavers." Moreover, when the ordinance was put in practice, they could no longer comply with the requests of foreign tapestry merchants who sent drawings of marks to be reproduced on new tapestry sets. The execution of this edict would not only dissatisfy the tapestry merchants but also prevent the sale of Antwerp tapestries. The Antwerp weavers also disagreed with the order that tapestries from the same series must be woven in the same town, provided that each of the pieces bore its own city mark. They therefore tried to prevent the publication of the ordinance in Antwerp. After a long dispute, Archduke Albert VII and Archduchess Isabella forced the Antwerp weavers "not to make or interweave anymore the *B*, *BB* or the red shield" and to come to an agreement with their Brussels colleagues.[35] Abuses continued, as shown by a notarial document of

1626.[36] Merchants as well as weavers interfered with the marks. Striking proof of this is revealed in the correspondence of 1708 between the art merchant Marcus Forchondt of Antwerp and his brother Justus in Vienna.[37] To make sure that they received orders for the tapestries, they not only cut out the workshops' marks from the borders and replaced them with black selvages, but also painted over the weavers' signatures, although the latter practice was not always successful.

The earlier general edict of 1544 was also put in practice in Grammont (Dutch: Geraardsbergen). This is confirmed by marks on tapestries consisting of a cross on three steps, which are derived from the city's coat of arms.[38] Some of these pieces also have the mark of the workshop in which they were woven. No city or workshop marks presently correspond to tapestry workshops of other weaving centers in the southern Netherlands, such as Leuven, Aalst, and Ieper.

In addition to city marks and marks or signatures of weavers, signatures of cartoon painters also exist on tapestries. This custom apparently originated in the seventeenth century. The oldest known example, dated 1644, is that of Lucas van Uden (1595–1672), an Antwerp artist whose name is interwoven on a verdure in the Schlossmuseum of Linz.[39] The signatures of other cartoon painters, such as Nicolaas van der Horst (1585–1646), Jan van den Hoecke (1611–1651), David Teniers II, David Teniers III, and Lodewijk Van Schoor are also found on tapestries.[40]

Typology: Outlook and Evolution

Until now, no systematic study has been made of the appearance of marks on tapestries. It is essential to offer a methodical study regarding the typology of marks to correctly resolve questions of date, authenticity, and identification. One can ascertain that the marks are interwoven in the tapestry to which they belong.[41] Most of the city and weavers' marks of the southern Netherlands appear in the selvages, especially in the lower border and in the lower corner of the right side

border. The selvages of large tapestries are often damaged as a result of handling, aging, or having been chewed by rodents, which cause the total or partial loss of marks. As the marks are an integral part of the textile, treatments for their conservation present problems similar to those for textiles. In the past they may have been rewoven, more or less exactly, during repair to the torn or damaged selvages. Normally a photograph will not allow us to see whether or not a mark has been rewoven; direct examination is often required. A related problem is the way marks have been placed on a series. A city and/or a weaver's mark will hardly ever be found on each tapestry of a complete set. Perhaps the weavers were not obliged to mark every piece of a set, or the marks may have been lost later by replacement of the selvages. When the selvages have not been replaced but simply folded back and hidden by a lining, it is possible to "rediscover" marks by removal of the lining.

Most marks are woven in wool, as is the greater part of the tapestry. For some, silk, even silver or gold threads were used. These more precious threads usually appear on sixteenth-century tapestries, especially in weavings from Brussels.[42] The marks were rendered mostly in light colors, in contrast to the dark background of the selvages (blue, green, or wine red).

3. City mark of Antwerp, *Grotesque with Nebuchadnezzar and the Young Men in the Fiery Furnace*, last quarter of the sixteenth century, tapestry
Rijksmuseum, Amsterdam, inv. no. RBK 1954–70

This emphasizes the importance of the photographic reproduction of a mark; in contrast to a drawing, where the dark outlines of the mark appear on a light ground, a photograph gives the realistic image of the mark.

The weavers never made a slavish copy of the city mark or that of the workshop. They apparently knew which characters or signs had to be included in the mark and sometimes represented them rather freely. Numerous variants of marks, differing slightly in form and dimension, often exist from the same city, or even the same workshop. These differences can even be found within one set.[43]

The technical aspects of weaving a tapestry further complicate the interpretation of a workshop's mark. A tapestry design is woven from side to side, which means that the design and the marks are woven at a ninety-degree angle from the viewing position. The mark was also intended to appear upright, vertically, at the right side of the tapestry, as viewed. This orientation of weaver and design made errors possible. It explains why workshop marks may appear upside down and/or on the left border, as is the case in one of the armorial tapestries of Charles V from the famous workshop of Willem de Pannemaker (Vienna, Kunsthistorishes Museum).[44] This can lead to a misreading of the mark by art historians. A monogram of an unidentified Brussels workshop, active about 1550, was misinterpreted by M. Calberg as *C.L.E.N.* and therefore attributed to the widow of Nicolaas Leyniers, Catharina van den Eynde. However, this sign is practically always reversed on the existing tapestries and should be read as *F.E.V.G.*, which makes the existence of the "widow Leyniers" very hypothetical.[45]

This example brings us to a new problem, the morphological evolution of the marks. When the city and workshop marks became compulsory (first in Brussels in 1528 and, after the publication of the imperial edict in 1544, in the other centers of the southern Netherlands), the marks were given a defined shape, which later changed in some cases. The Brussels city mark often served as a model for other city marks: in the middle, the shield of the town, flanked by two initials. The two *B*s, the abbreviation of Brabant-Brussels (see fig. 1),[46] indicated the province, followed by the name of the city. This was first imitated in Antwerp (*B-A*, Brabant-Antwerp) (see fig. 3) and later in workshops of emigrant Flemish weavers who had to "invent" city marks of their own. An example is Frans Spiering in Delft, who used *H-D* to stand for Holland-Delft (fig. 4).[47] However, the two initials are mostly a formal imitation of the famous *B-B*; in Enghien, *E-N* indicates the first and last letter of the name of the town in Dutch (Edingen) as well as in French (Enghien) (fig. 5).[48] The duplication of the *B* was also occasionally used by Flemish weavers working abroad. At the beginning of the *arazzeria medicea* in Florence in 1545–1546, for example, they initially used the inscriptions *FA.FLO* and *FATTO IN FIORENZA* (made in Florence); they also used the initial *F-F* on either side of the Florentine lily.[49] No similar explanation can be found for the city mark of Paris, introduced at the beginning of the seventeenth century by the workshops of Coomans and Van der Plancken, namely, the initials *P-P*, surrounding the French lily.[50]

The weavers' marks underwent a very complex evolution, which will be discussed only briefly. From the inception of tapestry marking in the second quarter of the sixteenth century to the beginning of the seventeenth century, the identification marks of the weavers' workshops or those of the contractors who were responsible for weaving the tapestries appeared next to the city marks. These weavers' marks were mainly composed as monograms, in which two or more letters of the name of the weaver-merchant were put side by side or entwined. They could be restricted to the initial of the first name of the weaver, to the initials of his first and family name, or they could contain several letters from both names (fig. 6). Other workshop marks often consisted of either the cipher *4* combined with letters or an abstract sign (fig. 7). Such marks can only be identified by fortunate discoveries in archives. Contemporary documents are also very helpful in deciphering monograms composed of initials. Proposed identification must meet certain requirements.

- The surname and first name of any individual weaver, as well as the period of his activity, must be clearly documented in archives.

- The initials and other letters of his name can be found in the monograms of tapestries whose style points to an origin of the same period.

- The group of letters can unequivocally be ascribed to one specific weaver of this period; the existence of two persons with the same initials, of course, weakens the hypothesis.[51]

Gradually the monograms began to include a greater number of characters and therefore became more complex. A probable explanation of this increase in characters is the fact that members of one family directed a workshop for several generations. This is confirmed by a list of Brussels weavers probably drafted shortly after 1600.[52] It explains why monograms, which were sometimes very complex and

6. Monogram of the Brussels weaver Cornelius Mattens, *The Battle of Troy*, c. 1600, tapestry

Royal Museums of Art and History, Brussels, inv. no. V2923 (Bequest of G. Vermeersch 1911). Photo A.C.L. Brussels

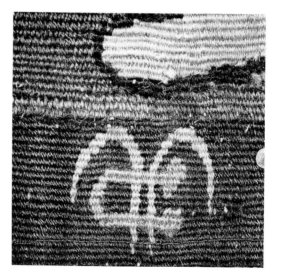

7. Unidentified weaver's mark, *Verdure*, second quarter of the sixteenth century, tapestry of Enghien

Royal Museums of Art and History, Brussels, inv. no. 3661. Photo A.C.L. Brussels

therefore very difficult to weave, were gradually abandoned in favor of initials, placed side by side, or even signatures partly or completely written in full.[53] Monograms and signatures can also be found on the same tapestry, for example on several pieces by the Brussels weaver Frans van Maelsaeck during the first third of the seventeenth century (fig. 8).[54]

8. (a) Monogram and (b) signature of the Brussels weaver Frans van Maelsaeck, *The Negotiations between Scipio and Hannibal*, c. 1629, Brussels tapestry
Royal Museums of Art and History, Brussels, inv. no. 8853. Photos A.C.L. Brussels

Nevertheless, several problems remain regarding the identification of these later "signatures" and, consequently, the chronology of production.[55] We can conclude that in Brussels, from the middle of the seventeenth century until the end of the eighteenth century, initials were used almost exclusively in combination with names written in full.

The signatures of the artists, not only the designers but also the cartoon painters, were woven in the same way. The first name and surname are often followed by such terms as *pinxit, invenit,* or *delineavit.* This form of signature is also found in engraving, another art form dependent on reproduction. It is probably not mere chance that the manner of signing was similar, as artists such as Nicolaas van der Horst and Jan van den Hoecke were also active as engravers.[56]

From the formal evolution of workshop marks, some conclusions about the topography of marks on tapestries can be formulated. Depending on the period and production center, the marks were indeed designated for a specific location on the tapestry. In Brussels, from the inception of marking in 1528 to the end of the century, the mark of the workshop was interwoven "on the one side" at the beginning of the work. After an inspection of the tapestry by the weavers' guild, the city mark was placed "on the other side" of the piece. As most of the existing Brussels tapestries of the sixteenth century have a weaver's mark on their right side border and the city mark on the left side of the lower border, we can deduce that the Brussels weavers very often started on the back of the right side.[57]

If two contractors were responsible for weaving a tapestry series, the marks of both of them are inserted on the series. The way in which they appear varies: the weavers' marks can be found on the same tapestry, where they usually appear above each other in the right side border, or the marks alternate on different pieces of the set.[58] When the weavers' monograms in a vertical form were gradually replaced by initials and signatures of a horizontal type, the placement of the signatures also changed, moving from the right vertical selvage border either to the right side border or often to the middle of the lower border. Brussels weavers of about 1700 were responsible for the last fundamental change in the placement of marks. At that time tapestry borders were no longer designed as mainly floral decoration, but as woven imitations of the gilded wood frames of paintings. The city and weavers' marks are frequently interwoven in the lower selvage, as before (fig. 8b), but often they are also found on the upper side of the woven frame or inside the figurative composition. In the latter case, the marks are mostly grouped on the right at the bottom. This is clearly an imitation of practices used by painters.

The imperial edict of 1544 was apparently very strictly applied in Enghien;

the city and weavers' marks are placed side by side in the lower border or upper selvage. The small number of city and weavers' marks from the rural centers of Oudenaarde and Grammont are mostly found in the lower selvage without the appearance of a formal order.

Bruges is a very special case. There the city mark underwent a particular evolution. At first, the crowned Gothic *B*, prescribed as the city mark by the municipality in 1547, was placed on the left in the lower border, just like the city marks of Brussels. This city mark disappeared for about one or two generations. By about 1575 it was replaced by the *broche*, the bobbin of the high-warp loom, which is found frequently in the middle of the right vertical selvage border. About 1630 the crowned *B* reappeared in the right selvage, together with the *broche*. In our opinion, the use of that instrument as an identification mark is an important argument for the existence of high-warp looms in Bruges.[59]

The total absence of marks from some centers of the southern Netherlands is unfortunate. According to the edict of 1544, towns such as Leuven, Mechelen, Sint-Truiden, and Ath also produced tapestries, so weavers there would also have been obliged to mark their products.[60]

Proposal for a New Synthesis

It is not the intention of this paper to present a complete survey of all publications about Flemish tapestries dealing with marks, monograms, and signatures of towns, workshops, and artists. Such a systematic study does not yet exist. This is one of the primary goals of our research and the proposed lexicon of marks.

The research about marks on Flemish tapestries began quite recently. Only since the last quarter of the nineteenth century have lists of such identification marks been given in art literature. A. Pinchart and A. Wauters were the founders of this study with their respective publications about marks of weavers from Oudenaarde and Brussels.[61] Other researchers at that time also published archival discoveries as well as marks, monograms, and signatures

9. Inscription of the cartoon painter Knoest, *The Finding of the Cross*, c. 1510, Brussels tapestry
Royal Museums of Art and History, Brussels, inv. no. 2993. Photo A.C.L. Brussels

on then-existing tapestries.[62] E. Muentz deserves special mention as the first to make a classification of such signs on some ninety tapestries from Brussels, Bruges, and other Flemish cities.[63] Expanding the research, in 1923 H. Goebel published the first volume of *Wandteppiche. Die Niederlande*, which includes an extended list of the marks, monograms, and signatures he found on Flemish tapestries.[64] Many of these signs have subsequently been identified correctly in numerous articles.[65] Also very important were archival discoveries of M. Crick-Kuntziger.[66]

The published lists, very valuable for their time, are now often out of date. The marks, monograms, and signatures are mostly presented as line drawings, which give a negative image of the actual mark. Numerous attributions have turned out to be incorrect or misinterpreted, and, as a consequence, many of the attributions are incomplete. M. Gebarowicz and T. Mankowski were the first to present marks by means of photographs, which are more truthful to the object.[67] Their example has been followed in most of the scientific catalogues of museums and exhibitions, as well as in specialized articles.[68]

There is no doubt that a new synthesis of marks on Flemish tapestries is needed. Some years ago the project of drafting a systematic study was conceived according to contemporary research criteria for art history.[69] Our intention is to produce a publication, with as many photographs as possible, of all the existing and available marks on old Flemish tapestries.

This lexicon of city marks, monograms, initials, and signatures of workshops and artists, including all the known variants, will then be accessible to researchers, art dealers, and art collectors. The intention is not to identify all of these signs and marks—a goal that probably would never be possible—but to make it possible to locate them with regard to place and time. All opinions mentioned in the specialized literature must be taken into account. The period of activity of every workshop or artist will be briefly stated; the most representative existing tapestries or tapestry series that illustrate the mark will be included in the dictionary, along with references to those that have been published and illustrated in accessible literature. References to the relevant existing literature will be given at the end of each entry. As the first edition of such a lexicon will inevitably be incomplete, it will not claim to be a corpus of Flemish tapestry.

A special documentation form has been designed (see appendix, this essay) and, since 1981, has been used to collect information on the marks, monograms, and signatures.[70] Hundreds of positive replies to this initial international inquiry have been received. We welcome and appreciate any new contributions from museum curators, art dealers, and collectors.

NOTES

1. Alphonse Wauters, *Les tapisseries bruxelloises. Essai historique sur les tapisseries de haute et de basse-lisse de Bruxelles* (Brussels, 1878), 148. The ordinance was published *in extenso* on pages 144–149. Prior to the edict of 1528, some Brussels tapestries had an inscription indicating their origin, namely the city (*BRUESEL*), the weaver and merchant (*AELST*), and the cartoon painter (*KNOEST*) (fig. 9). See Jan Karel Steppe, "Inscriptions décoratives contenant des signatures et des mentions du lieu d'origine sur des tapisseries bruxelloises de la fin du xve et du début du xvie siècle," in *Tapisseries bruxelloises de la pré-Renaissance* [exh. cat., Musées Royaux d'Art et d'Histoire] (Brussels, 1976), 193–231. This contribution is partly based on the work of A. De Decker, *Sierteksten in de kunst van de Zuidelijke Nederlanden,* M.A. thesis, dactylographies, Katholieke Universiteit, Leuven, 1963.

2. Wauters 1878, 37–40. Because of the existence of some tapestries older than 1528 with the Brussels city mark (e.g., in La Seo, Saragossa), Steppe in Brussels 1976, 195, conjectured that the tradition of interweaving the city mark may have existed in Brussels before the publication of the ordinance. He raised the question of whether Brussels weavers and merchants had to add the city mark on pieces woven or finished before 16 May 1528.

3. The fact that seals were attached to the tapestries can be deduced from a document of 1472: "Therefore one should bring the above-mentioned pieces in the chapel of Saint Christophorus, just as it was the custom to attach the mentioned seal on them before" (translated according to Wauters 1878, 42).

4. Joseph Destrée, *L'Industrie de la tapisserie à Enghien et dans la Seigneurie de ce nom* (Enghien, 1900), 9. In 1513, Philip of Cleve imposed the regulations on the weavers' guild of Enghien. The most important articles concerning the sealing are numbered 16, 18, and 19.

5. Jan Karel Steppe, "Enkele nieuwe gegevens betreffende tapijtwerk van de Geschiedenis van Vertumnus en Pomona vervaardigd door Willem de Pannemaker voor Filips ii van Spanje," in *Artes Textiles* 10 (1981), 136 and fig. 2.

6. Wauters 1878, 41.

7. Wauters 1878, 46.

8. See also section on "Typology: Outlook and Evolution" in text.

9. Wauters 1878, 148.

10. Alphonse Wauters, "Les tapisseries de Bruxelles et leurs marques," in *L'Art* 26 (1881), 108.

11. Important discoveries are the documents from 1576 and the first quarter of the seventeenth century, which give the identification of some tens of marks: Fernand Donnet, "Les tapisseries de Bruxelles, Enghien et Audenarde pendant la Furie espagnole (1576)," in *Annales de la Société d'Archéologie de Bruxelles* 8 (1894), 451–452. Marthe Crick-Kuntziger, "Marques et signatures de tapissiers bru-

xellois," in *Annales de la Société royale d'Archéologie de Bruxelles* 40 (1936), 175–177, 179–180, published the document of 2 August 1610 with four marks, as well as a document of 27 January 1614 with seven marks, one of which had already been published in 1610. Another document of 1614 gives twenty-five marks, of which two had previously been published and another two cannot be identified. Crick-Kuntziger 1936, 180–181, identified fourteen marks, and the document was published by Nora De Poorter, "The Eucharist Series," vol. 2 of *Corpus Rubenianum Ludwig Burchard*, 2 vols. (Brussels, 1978), 2: pl. 38.

12. Guy Delmarcel, *Tapisseries anciennes d'Enghien* (Mons, 1980), 8–9.

13. Sophie Schneebalg-Perelman, "'Le retouchage' dans la tapisserie bruxelloise ou les origines de l'édit impérial de 1544," in *Annales de la Société Royale d'Archéologie de Bruxelles* 50 (1961), 4–5.

14. The edict of 1544 has been published by G. T. van Ysselsteyn, *Geschiedenis der tapijtweverijen in de Noordelijke Nederlanden. Bijdragen tot de geschiedenis der kunstnijverheid*, 2 vols. (Leyden, 1936), 2:1–21 (art. 41 on p. 9). The ordinance was published in French by J. Lameere and H. Simont, *Recueil des ordonnances des Pays-Bas. Deuxième série. 1500–1700*, 5 (Brussels, 1910), 40–50.

15. According to article 85 of the edict, a weaver in the country could choose the mark he wanted, provided that he respected the instructions of the city he selected. We therefore agree with Martine Vanwelden, *Het tapijtweversambacht te Oudenaarde. 1441–1772* (Oudenaarde, 1979), 113, who states that, for the buyer, the term "tapestry work of Oudenaarde" indicated the quality of the piece rather than the place of origin. It should be mentioned that the weaver probably selected a neighboring tapestry center. A weaver living not far from the adjacent towns of Oudenaarde and Grammont would probably have preferred the city mark of one of these towns.

16. This is stated in article 89 of the edict: "Nobody, whoever he is, will demand him to make, to falsify, or to remove the mark of another weaver. If the weaver breaks this rule, he will not only have his right hand cut off but also be interdicted from the guild of weavers and from the trade of tapestries" (translated according to van Ysselsteyn 1936, 20).

17. Adolphe Hullebroeck, *Histoire de la tapisserie à Audenarde du XVe au XVIIIe siècle* (Renaix, 1939), 30; Vanwelden 1979, 113.

18. See van Ysselsteyn 1936, 15, for article 67 of the edict.

19. Vanwelden 1979, 59.

20. Vanwelden 1979, 73, mentions the lawsuit of 1640 against Jan Baert, accused of falsification of the mark.

21. The date of the publication is mentioned only by the French edition of Lameere and Simont 1910, 50.

22. Wauters 1878, 211, 228.

23. Jacqueline Versyp, *De geschiedenis van de tapijtkunst te Brugge*, vol. 8 of *Verhandelingen van de Koninklijke Vlaamse Academie voor Wetenschappen, Letteren en Schone Kunsten van België. Klasse der Schone Kunsten* (Brussels, 1954), 203, published the document of 2 May 1547 in which it is mentioned that the imperial edict, with the *in extenso*-cited article 41, has been published "in the abovementioned town of Bruges." We rectify here our incorrect statement that the mark of the workshop was not mentioned in the ordinance of Bruges: see Guy Delmarcel, "Marques et techniques dans les tapisseries brugeoises," Guy Delmarcel and Erik Duverger in *Bruges et la tapisserie* [exh. cat., Gruuthusemuseum and Memlingmuseum] (Bruges, 1987), 145.

24. Delmarcel and Duverger in Bruges 1987, 139–140.

25. J. Denucé, *Les tapisseries anversoises. Fabrication et commerce*, vol. 4 of *Sources pour l'histoire de l'art flamand* (Antwerp, 1936), 21: "On which respect those of the town of Ghent also are obliged to publish the above-mentioned ordinance in Ghent, as it was decided by the Secret Council on the last day of September" (translation).

26. Heinrich Goebel, *Wandteppiche. Die Niederlande*, 2 vols. (Leipzig, 1923). In the list of marks in 1:20, an example is given of a tapestry in the state collection of Bavaria depicting *The Last Supper*. It is still questionable if this piece was woven in Ghent.

27. See Erik Duverger, *Jan, Jacques en Frans de Moor, tapijtwevers en tapijthandelaars te Oudenaarde, Antwerpen en Gent (1560 tot ca. 1680)*, vol. 1 of *Interuniversitair Centrum voor de geschiedenis van de Vlaamse tapijtkunst. Verhandelingen en bouwstoffen* (Ghent, 1960), 321–322; Jozef Duverger, "Adriaen van der Gracht (c. 1520–1575). Een bijdrage tot de tapijtnijverheid te Gent in het midden van de 16de eeuw," in *Artes Textiles* 8 (1974), 37.

28. Denucé 1936, xix–xx, 19–20 (document 5).

29. Wauters 1878, 175.

30. Wauters 1878, 175, wrote of a re-edition. There is a question as to whether the edict published earlier was ever put in practice.

31. Erik Duverger, *Antwerpse wandtapijten* [exh. cat., Het Sterckshof] (Deurne, 1973), 22–23.

32. Wauters 1878, 172–175.

33. Denucé 1936, 42–50.

34. Denucé 1936, 50–52.

35. Documents concerning this dispute and the final agreement have been published by Denucé 1936, 52–58.

36. Erik Duverger, "La marque de la ville de Bruxelles sur des tapisseries anversoises," in *Artes Textiles* 10 (1981), 296–297, note 14.

37. J. Denucé, *Exportation d'oeuvres d'art au 17e siècle à Anvers. La firme Forchoudt*, vol. 1 of *Sources pour l'histoire de l'art flamand* (Antwerp, 1929), 267–268.

38. Goebel 1923, 501, and list of marks, 20.

39. Isabelle Van Tichelen, *Patroonschilders voor Vlaamse wandtapijten werkzaam te Brussel en te Antwerpen tijdens de zeventiende eeuw*, M.A. thesis, dactylographies, Katholieke Universiteit, Leuven, 1986), 112–113.

40. Van Tichelen 1986, 48, 54.

41. In some very rare cases (e.g., in the workshop of Jan Raes, c. 1600) tapestry marks were embroidered, mostly as a copy of a monogram already woven on another place.

42. See, for example, *The Grotesque Months* and *The Life of Moses* in the Kunsthistorisches Museum, Vienna; Elisabeth Mahl, "Die 'Mosesfolge' der Tapisseriensammlung des Kunsthistorischen Museums in Wien," in *Jahrbuch der Kunsthistorischen Sammlungen in Wien* 69 (1973), 55–84.

43. Guy Delmarcel and Claire Dumortier, "Cornelis de Ronde, wandtapijtwever te Brussel (+1569)," in *Revue Belge d'Archéologie et d'Histoire de l'art* 55 (1986), 43, fig. 1. The questionnaire on the dictionary of marks (see appendix, this essay) also requests the dimensions of the marks (height and width in cm): these statistics have not yet been compiled.

44. Ernst von Birk, "Inventar der im Besitz des Allerhoechsten Kaiserhauses befindlichen Niederlaender Tapeten und Gobelins," in *Jahrbuch der Kunsthistorischen Sammlungen des Allerhoechstes Kaiserhauses* 1 (1883), 240.

45. Marguerite Calberg, "Episodes de l'Histoire des saints Pierre et Paul. Tapisseries de Bruxelles tissées au XVIe siècle pour l'abbaye Saint-Pierre à Gand," in *Bulletin des Musées Royaux d'Art et d'Histoire* 34 (1962), 105–108. The mark is represented in its correct position in *Tapisseries flamandes du château du Wawel à Cracovie et d'autres collections européennes* [exh. cat., Sint-Pietersabdij] (Ghent, 1986–1987), 28–29, 38. This inversion was previously noticed by Nora De Poorter, "Over de weduwe Geubels en de datering van Jordaens' tapijtenreeks 'De taferelen uit het landleven,'" in *Gentse Bijdragen tot de Kunstgeschiedenis* 25 (1979–1980), 216, note 25.

46. See the document of 1617 about the dispute between the weavers of Brussels and Antwerp: "The Brussels weavers always use on their tapestries the two *B*s and between them a red shield, that is to say, the first *B* is an indication for Brabant and the second one for Brussels" (translation according to Denucé 1936, 44).

47. Guy Delmarcel, *Tapisseries. Renaissance et Maniérisme* [mus. guide, Musées Royaux d'Art et d'Histoire] (Brussels, 1979), pls. 26 and 41.

48. For examples, see Delmarcel 1980, 69, 82.

49. These inscriptions, and later the initials on both

sides of the lily, were introduced by two Flemish weavers, Nicolaas Karcher and Jan Rost, who left Mantova and Ferrara, respectively, for Florence in 1545. See Candace Adelson, "Cosimo 1 de' Medici and the Foundation of Tapestry Production in Florence," in vol. 3 of *Firenze e la Toscana dei Medici nell' Europa del '500* (Florence, 1983), 912–913, note 41. For illustrations, see Goebel 1923, list of marks, 15. Also in Ferrara, Jan (Giovanni) Karcher signed with the inscription *FACTUM FERRARIAE* in 1545 (*Metamorphoses* after Battista Dossi, now in the Louvre, Paris), as well as in 1552 and 1553 (*Lives of the Saints George and Maurelius* [Museo della Cattedrale, Ferrara]). See Nello Forti Grazzini, *L'Arazzo ferrarese* (Ferrara, 1982), 107, 115.

50. Goebel 1923, list of marks, 1 and 2; Jean Coural, *Chefs-d'oeuvre de la tapisserie parisienne* [exh. cat., Versailles, Orangerie] (Versailles, 1967), 107.

51. Delmarcel and Dumortier 1986, 41–42.

52. See note 11.

53. See examples in Rotraud Bauer and Guy Delmarcel, *Tapisseries bruxelloises au siècle de Rubens* [exh. cat., Musées Royaux d'Art et d'Histoire] (Brussels, 1977), 44–59, 70–82.

54. For Jan Raes, see Guy Delmarcel, "L'Arazzeria antica a Bruxelles e la manifattura di Jan Raes," in *Arazzi per la cattedrale di Cremona* [exh. cat., Santa Maria della Pietà] (Cremona, 1987), 45–46, figs. 32–43.

55. De Poorter 1979–1980, 208–224 and Erik Duverger, "Enkele archivalische gegevens over Catharina van den Eynde en over haar zoon Jacques II Geubels, tapissiers te Brussel," in *Gentse Bijdragen tot de Kunstgeschiedenis* 26 (1981–1984), 161–193.

56. See Brussels 1977, 70, *Johannes van den Hoecke inv. et pinxit*; see also Hans Vlieghe, "David Teniers II en David Teniers III als patroonschilders voor de tapijtweverijen," in *Artes Textiles* 5 (1959–1960), 86–88, and Van Tichelen 1986, 112–113. In rare cases one can also find the name of the dealer (e.g., *GILLIS.GEROBO HOEFHANDL* on the tapestries of the Eucharist series in Vienna, KHM CV8/1–3) or signs placed at the time of a restoration (e.g., the Lotharingian cross of the Moses series in Vienna, KHM I/1–9).

57. Delmarcel and Duverger in Bruges 1987, 139–140.

58. Examples of alternating marks are seen in series of tapestries woven in the workshops of Raes and Geubels at the end of the sixteenth century, the *Acts of the Apostles* and the *Life of Alexander*, both in the Spanish Royal Collection. See Paulina Junquera de Vega, Concha Herrero Carretero, and Carmen Dias Gallegos, *Catálogo de tapices del Patrimonio Nacional*, 2 vols. (Madrid, 1986), 1:248–262, 2:62–74.

59. Delmarcel and Duverger in Bruges 1987, 141.

60. In drafting his lists of marks, Heinrich Goebel, the great historian of the European art of tapestry, has invented too much for all of these centers; imi-

tating the marks known for other cities, which usually contain the city coat of arms, he "designed" city marks for these centers using their respective coats of arms. (Goebel 1923, list of marks, 18, 20–21).

61. A. Pinchart, *Histoire générale de la tapisserie. Pays-Bas* (Paris, 1878–1884), 109, and Alphonse Wauters, "Les tapisseries de Bruxelles et leurs marques," in *L'Art* 26 (1881), 241–245; 27 (1881), 25–35, 108–109, 221–225, 241–244. Separate marks had already been published: Alfred Darcel, "Union Centrale des Beaux-Arts appliqués à l'industrie. Musée rétrospectif. Le Moyen-Age et la Renaissance," in *Gazette des Beaux-Arts*, 1 series, 20 (1866), 75; Alfred Darcel, "Union Centrale des Beaux-Arts appliqués à l'industrie. Exposition de l'histoire de la tapisserie," in *Gazette des Beaux-Arts*, 2 series, 14 (1876), 48–77; *Collection de S. A. le duc de Berwick et d'Albe* (sales cat., Hôtel Drouot, Paris, 7–20 April 1877).

62. We cite only von Birk 1883, 213–248, and von Birk, "Inventar der im Besitz des Allerhoechsten Kaiserhauses befindlichen Niederlaender Tapeten und Gobelins," in *Jahrbuch der Kunsthistorischen Sammlungen des Allerhoechsten Kaiserhauses* 2 (1884), 167–220; W. G. Thomson, *A History of Tapestry* (London, 1906), 472–480.

63. Eugène Muentz, "Notes sur l'histoire de la tapisserie. Monogrammes et marques de tapissiers," in *La Chronique des Arts* (1888), 190–191, 205–206.

64. Goebel 1923.

65. Some examples from before World War II: John Boettiger, *Tapisseries à figures des XVIᵉ et XVIIᵉ siècles appartenant à des collections privées de la Suède. Inventaire descriptif* (Stockholm, 1928); van Ysselsteyn 1936, 2:477–487; Marthe Crick-Kuntziger, "Tapisseries de la Genèse d'après Michel Coxcie," in *Bulletin de la Société Royale d' Archéologie de Bruxelles* 1 (1938), 5–17; Hullebroeck 1939, 41–44.

66. See note 11.

67. M. Gebarowicz and T. Mankowski, *Arasy Zygmunta Augusta*, vol. 24 of *Rocznik Krakowski* (Cracow, 1937).

68. Marthe Crick-Kuntziger, *Musées Royaux d'Art et d'Histoire de Bruxelles. Catalogue des tapisseries (XIVᵉ au XVIIIᵉ siècle)* (Brussels, 1956), pl. 120; Adolph S. Cavallo, *Tapestries of Europe and Colonial Peru in the Museum of Fine Arts, Boston* 2 (Boston, 1967), pl. 1; Nello Forti Grazzini, *Museo d'Arti Applicate. Arazzi (Musei e Gallerie di Milano)* (Milan, 1984), 203–204; Rotraud Bauer, *Tapisserien im Zeichen der Kunst Raffaels* [exh. cat., Reitschule der Hofstallungen] (Vienna, 1983).

69. Guy Delmarcel, "Marks and Monograms on Ancient Flemish Tapestries. Outlines for a Lexicon," in *Bulletin de Liaison du Centre international d'étude des textiles anciens* 53 (1981), 56–59.

70. See appendix, this essay.

APPENDIX

MARKS ON ANCIENT FLEMISH TAPESTRIES

MARK—MONOGRAM—SIGNATURE

(Please attach here picture or drawing,
or refer to it)

1. **IDENTIFICATION** (weaver/artist)_____

2. **MARK—MONOGRAM—SIGNATURE**

2.1 Dimensions (height x width, in
centimeters):_____

2.2 Material: wool☐ silk☐ silver☐ gold☐

2.3 Color:_____

2.4 Authenticity: original☐ restored☐
rewoven☐

2.5 Location. Please locate mark on the scheme:
s. = selvage; b. = border;
c. = central field
Please note distance of mark from
nearest corner in centimeters.

3. **TAPESTRY**

3.1 Name of tapestry series:_____

3.2 Name of single tapestry, where mark appears:_____

3.3 Dimensions of tapestry (h. x w., in centimeters):_____

3.4 Place and date of manufacture:_____

3.5 Designer:_____

3.6 Actual owner:_____

3.7 Inventory number:_____

3.8 Actual location (if different from 3.6):_____

3.9 Provenance:_____

3.10 Bibliography: Please cite the most recent and/or comprehensive references; if the
tapestry or the series is illustrated, add *"ill."*

(use separate sheet if necessary)

Please send this form to: Prof. Guy Delmarcel, Bergstraat 150, 3010 Leuven, Belgium

LILIANE MASSCHELEIN-KLEINER

Study and Treatment of Tapestries at the Institut Royal du Patrimoine Artistique

It is well known that tapestries are an important part of Europe's cultural heritage, especially that of Belgium. For several centuries the brilliant weavings of the manufactories of Tournai, Brussels, Bruges, Antwerp, Oudenaarde, and Enghien were sold throughout the world. A rich patrimony of tapestries also remains in Belgium, particularly in official buildings, museums, castles, and churches, for which the Institut Royal du Patrimoine Artistique in Brussels provides assistance. A principle in our work is respect for the authenticity of each art object. Before beginning any treatment, art historians, scientists, and conservators collaborate in a basic study of the object. It is necessary to identify not only the tapestry's historic, aesthetic, sociological, and technical meanings but also its materials, as well as the presence of alterations and the techniques used in making these alterations. The best approach to conservation, in order to achieve a favorable balance between the object's original state and present condition, is jointly determined in this preliminary study.

Efforts to conserve tapestries were begun some twenty years ago. We began with the classical reweaving method then in use in most workshops. Gradually our approach changed, and, at the present time, we tend more often to limit treatment to strict conservation.

Gobelins Manufactory, *La fenaison* (detail), seventeenth century, tapestry
Ministry of the French Community of Belgium, Seneffe Castle

Technical Study

Fibers and Texture

From the fifteenth to the nineteenth centuries, the warps of Belgian-made tapestries were made of undyed wool spun in Z-twist and plied in S-twist. In Tournai the warps in the fifteenth century were mostly 3-ply, with a shift to 2-ply in the sixteenth century; in Brussels and Antwerp they were often 3-ply; in Bruges and Oudenaarde they were either 2-ply or 3-ply.

In the sixteenth century the Tournai tapestries became coarser, 4–5 warp threads per centimeter being used compared with 5–6 warp threads per centimeter in the fifteenth century. Brussels tapestries are remarkably fine, 7.25–8.25 and more warp threads per centimeter. In Antwerp and Bruges the texture grew finer, changing from 5–6 warp threads in the sixteenth century to 7–8 by the end of the seventeenth century. This phenomenon is attributed to the tendency of tapestry weavers at that time to imitate oil paintings. Generally the wefts are made of wool or silk double threads. The metallic threads have a silk core along which a silver or a gilded silver strip 0.2–6.0 millimeter wide is coiled in S-twist.[1]

Dyeing Techniques

For several years we have analyzed dyestuffs using thin-layer chromatogra-

71

phy, an inexpensive analytical method that allows a rapid identification of minute samples.[2] High-performance liquid chromatography (HPLC) has been introduced recently.[3] Coupled with ultraviolet-visible spectroscopy or mass-spectrometry, it permits qualitative and quantitative analyses of several dyestuffs with a single injection of the sample.

All our analyses yield the same conclusions regarding the importance of the guilds' regulations up to the middle of the seventeenth century. Following this period, new dyes that were either not allowed or unknown in the Middle Ages were increasingly used, and an expanded range of shades, made from sophisticated mixtures of all the dyes, was introduced.

In the first period regulated by the guilds the red shades were generally achieved with madder (*Rubia tinctorum*). This dyestuff was used alone or mixed with weld (*Reseda luteola*), brazilwood (*Caesalpina* species), and occasionally kermes (*Kermes vermilio*). The dyestuff was fixed on the fiber with alum mordant for the light colors and iron mordant for the dark colors. Brazilwood was tolerated only for shading a fast dye because of its poor lightfastness. We found it only in Antwerp tapestries, where the guild regulations were apparently less rigorous.

Using HPLC, Jan Wouters discovered an interesting variation in the proportion of alizarin to purpurin in some madder dyes.[4] This ratio varies from 65:35 to 20:80, producing a wide range of colors from orange-red to carmine. This variation was particularly characteristic of tapestries from Bruges. It is not yet known how these wonderful red hues were achieved by the dyers. They could have extracted the dyes or mixed different species of plants (*Rubia peregrina, munjista*). Cochineal (*Coccus cacti*) became very fashionable at the end of the seventeenth century, especially "cochineal scarlet," which was made using a tin mordant. This was used in Antwerp and Bruges before it was introduced in Brussels. In the seventeenth century, tannins were increasingly used alone to form brown, as well as in combination with every other dye. This practice was forbidden during the Middle Ages.

Archil (*Rocella tinctoria*) was also strongly forbidden in the Middle Ages because of its sensitivity to light. However, this poor-quality dye was used later and did prove to fade quickly.

Weld was the only yellow dyestuff allowed by the guilds in Flanders and Artois. Other yellow dyestuffs such as old fustic (*Chlorophora tinctoria*), young fustic (*Rhus cotinus*), and turmeric (*Curcuma longa*) were used in Brussels and Antwerp tapestries from the end of the seventeenth century. Old fustic was also used in Bruges.

The blue colors were made of indigo until the eighteenth century. The regulations favored the use of the indigenous woad (*Isatis tintoria*) over the *indigoferae* species, which had to be imported; nevertheless, the presence of indirubin in a few samples indicates the use of the latter. Weld and madder were often added to indigo in the Bruges tapestries, probably in order to promote the fermentation of the vat, although they also influenced the resulting colors. In 1740, indigo carmine, the sulfonated indigo, was prepared by Barth and soon replaced indigo for the blue dyes because it is water soluble and therefore much easier to use. Unfortunately it, too, is not lightfast, causing strong fading of the blue shades.

The other colors such as orange, green, purple, and brown are the results of mixtures of the above dyestuffs. New metallic mordants such as copper or chromium also came into use in the middle of the eighteenth century.

Mauvein, the first synthetic dyestuff, was discovered by William Henry Perkin in 1858. This was quickly followed by a whole range of aniline compounds, a family of bright dyes that are not lightfast or washfast.

The use of these poor-quality dyestuffs was fortunately limited in tapestries. The Gobelins manufactory reports the use of synthetic dyes beginning only in 1911, when several better dyes such as the anthraquinones were synthesized. Nevertheless, unstable dyes were used in many restorations and now preclude wetcleaning.

It is known that dyeing techniques were better for the early tapestries. From the fifteenth century to the middle of the sev-

1. Vacuum cleaning of a tapestry. Both sides are cleaned through a screen in order to limit loss of threads

Treatment

Cleaning

Each time an old tapestry is wet- or dry-cleaned, a certain number of the original threads are unavoidably lost. This operation must therefore be used sparingly and delayed as long as possible by maintaining the tapestry in a clean atmosphere. The piece should periodically be vacuum cleaned on both sides, done very carefully with a screen barrier to limit the suction (fig. 1). When cleaning is absolutely necessary, a wet process is preferred because it can eliminate many kinds of soil and also relax stretching and restore flexibility to the fibers. Of course the washfastness of all colored materials, both the original and those used in any restorations, must be tested very carefully. We add just a small amount of non-ionic detergent (0.01–0.02 g per liter). We do not use any polyphosphates or carboxymethylcellulose because they have an affinity for the fibers and mordants and may have long-term damaging effects.[5] As the non-ionic detergent does not precipitate the calcium ions, we use ordinary tapwater for the first baths, while the last rinsing is carried out with demineralized water.

To assure that no trace of detergent remains on the textile, we use the "foam test" on the rinsing water. All these procedures are carried out as quickly as possible, after which the tapestry is dried with towels and blotting paper. The old fibers should not remain wet any longer than necessary because dampness promotes their further hydrolysis and may cause bleeding of the dyestuffs from the silk threads. The tapestry is then left to dry under slight tension, which is maintained by small lead blocks.

When unstable dyes or cotton threads preclude immersing the tapestry in water, we sometimes remove the dirt from the surface by gently dabbing both sides with damp sponges that are frequently rinsed with water (figs. 2a and 2b). If only dry cleaning is advisable, we use a specialized firm that performs work according to our requirements: (1) the textile must be kept flat; (2) the solvent is freshly distilled white spirit; (3) only a very small amount

enteenth, the tapestries were appreciated as monumental decorations. A fairly narrow range of shades was used in producing them, and the weaver had liberty in interpreting the designs. Later the number of shades significantly increased owing to the new fashion for tapestries whose palette imitated oil painting. Mixtures of four dyestuffs, and sometimes more, were needed to match exactly the colors of the painted cartoon. This is certainly one factor contributing to their extreme fading. The use of these unstable dye mixtures may unfavorably affect washfastness.

Another reason for avoiding wetcleaning is that some tapestries were embellished with touches of paint. This peculiar technique was found in a sixteenth-century Brussels tapestry titled *The Lamentation*. Traces of painting enhanced the flesh tones and underlined the eyes and lips. We were unable to find any binding medium with the pigments, which were principally ocher and carbon black. It is important, of course, to take care to preserve this valuable aesthetic and technical evidence.

of non-ionic detergent solution may be used, and only when absolutely necessary; and (4) friction is not permitted.

Consolidation

Gradually during the last decade reweaving has been eliminated because of a number of negative findings: (1) the new wool is much softer and more hairy than the original and does not mesh perfectly with the old parts; (2) anchorage of new warps creates tension and loss of original threads; (3) uneven fading of original and new materials may occur; (4) the new weaving would be difficult to remove should it become unattractive as it ages; and (5) reweaving of lost details often implies alteration of the original design. For these reasons, we rarely reweave and only do so when the lost design is very well known and simple (for example, a missing plain border) and useful for the conservation of the piece.

Consolidation begins with the sewing of open slits with blanket stitches from the back of the tapestry (fig. 3). Fragile areas are then reinforced by relining them with linen patches. At first we tried to consolidate the fragile areas by sewing loose warps and wefts onto local patches, using the laid and couching technique employed for other kinds of textiles. We found, however, that this procedure did not blend well with the texture of the tapestry and also was not strong enough to sustain the weight of the tapestry when hung.[6] After several mechanical tests, we decided to replace the laid and couching technique by alternating rows of stitches that follow the wefts.

Silk threads are chosen for sewing despite their sensitivity to ultraviolet light and stretching. Other fibers exhibit even more disadvantages: (1) wool lacks the desired luster and has a long extension at break; (2) mercerized cotton is much stronger than the original old fibers and has a tendency to shrink; (3) polyester is even stronger and, in contrast to the old natural fibers, is not at all hygroscopic; and (4) nylon is very damaging because of its scissoring effect. The silk threads are carefully dyed to avoid weakening them; we believe that our silk threads will thus have a rea-

sonable lifetime. Finally, it is our hope that when the tapestries we have treated are reinstalled in the gallery, the curator will take care that the lighting is free of ultraviolet rays and does not exceed 50 lux. Tapestries should hang no longer than six months at a time.

Patches and other linings are made of thin linen fabric weighing about 200 grams per square meter. Flax is the natural fiber with the highest breaking strength and the lowest extension at break, even after aging. These qualities are necessary to ensure that

2. (a) When unstable dyes preclude immersing the tapestry in water, it is still possible to take advantage of the action of water by dabbing both sides with damp sponges. (b) The drying is cautiously accelerated with cold air from hair dryers

3. Blanket stitches are used to sew slits, as seen from the reverse side of the tapestry

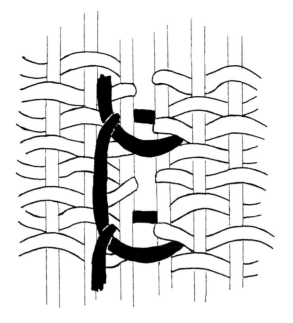

internal tensions that are responsible for shrinking. We dye the patches to match the colors of the surrounding area of the tapestry, using direct dyes with a very high light- and washfastness.

Old repairs are removed only when necessary for conservation, such as when they cause tension. Unsightly old restorations are often allowed to remain because their removal would damage the tapestry or because of time constraints.

The tapestry is then drawn on tracing paper. The areas of consolidation are determined and the future distribution of support stitches is precisely indicated on the paper. The patches are attached to the back of the tapestry with zigzag stitches. They extend beyond the damaged parts into stable areas. The tapestry is then stretched on a special frame (fig. 4), and the damaged areas are sewn on their individual lining patches with interrupted and overlapping rows of stitches, each about 4 centimeters long (fig. 5a). The silk sewing thread follows the wefts and is totally invisible from the front of the tapestry. Each time a stitch is made, the conservator

in time the lining will not be hanging from the tapestry instead of the reverse. This applies, of course, to a linen fabric of good quality made of long flax fibers. We thoroughly boil the fabric before use to eliminate any finishing products and to relax the

4. The frame is provided with three lifting jacks in order to regulate stretching throughout the length of the tapestry

indicates its position with a cross on the sketch. Exposed warps are aligned on the lining with a silk thread that follows the twist of the warp (fig. 5b).

For a long time the most delicate problem was the mending of large holes. The texture of the linen patch and its drape does not fit well aesthetically when it is visible over a large area. Juliette De boeck has found a very good solution; she imitates the missing part of the tapestry by embroidering warp- and weftlike threads on the linen patch.[7] The appearance is quite satisfying and the process is easily reversible.

Finally we line the whole reverse of a tapestry with the same fine linen fabric used for the patches. First, the lining and a wide band of Velcro™ are sewn at the same time onto the top reverse of the tapestry; second, the tapestry and lining are hung. Several conservators working at the front and the back then fasten the lining throughout the tapestry; working in pairs, they sew vertical rows of running stitches 45 centimeters long, spaced 15 centimeters apart. The vertical stitches pass over 2½ centimeters at the back and over one warp at the front. The sides are attached only along two-thirds of their length from the top. The bottom hangs loose to prevent it from sagging.

Adhesive Treatments

The gluing of tapestries has brought disastrous results.[8] Adhesives cause loss of flexibility, mechanical constraints, and yellowing; they attract dust and form harmful degradation products. In addition, adhesives are impossible to remove completely. When removal is attempted, there is always a considerable loss of yarn. The use of a glued net is pointless; it cannot sustain the weight of the tapestry, and some glue that cannot be completely eliminated always gets trapped in the fibers.

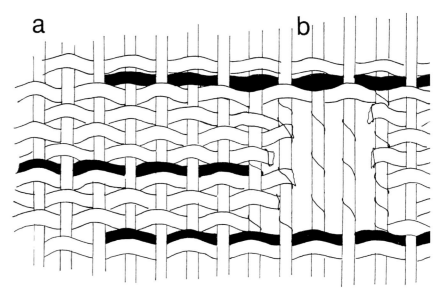

The removal of any residual glue requires the use of a large amount of solvent, a procedure extremely dangerous for both the textile and the conservators.

Conclusion

As with other art objects, tapestries must be treated carefully to preserve their authenticity. Handling a historical piece is a great responsibility. Prior to any decision on treatment, a thorough study of the tapestry is therefore essential, and it must be carried out with the collaboration of concerned scientists, art historians, and conservators. The treatment must be precisely proposed and documented by sketches and photographs. Each tapestry has its own unique problems that require special solutions. However, the same principles remain valid: the methods and the materials must be safe for the object, especially on a long-term basis; the treatment must be reversible as far as possible; and, most important of all, it should not misrepresent the original creation.

5. (a) Consolidation of fragile areas by sewing on linen patches, using short stabilizing wefts randomly distributed. (b) The blank warps are stitched on the lining with a silk thread that follows its twist direction

NOTES

1. René Lefève and Jozef Vynckier, "Etude technique de la tapisserie tournaisienne au xvᵉ siècle. La texture," *Bulletin de l'Institut Royal du Patrimoine Artistique* 11 (1969), 41–53; Lefève and Vynckier, "Etude technique de la tapisserie tournaisienne aux xvᵉ et xviᵉ siècles. La texture," *Bulletin de l'Institut Royal du Patrimoine Artistique* 12 (1970), 272–279; Lefève and Vynckier, "Etude technique de la tapisserie des Pays-Bas Méridionaux aux xvᵉ et xviᵉ siècles," *Bulletin de l'Institut Royal du Patrimoine Artistique* 14 (1973–1974), 195–198; Lefève and Vynckier, "Etude technique de la tapisserie des Pays-Bas Méridionaux. Les tapisseries anversoises des xviᵉ et xviiᵉ siècles. Le textile," *Bulletin de l'Institut Royal du Patrimoine Artistique* 16 (1976–1977), 147–152; Vynckier, "Etude technique de la tapisserie des Pays-Bas Méridionaux. Les tapisseries bruxelloises au siècle de Rubens," *Bulletin de l'Institut Royal du Patrimoine Artistique* 18 (1980–1981), 187–188.

2. Liliane Masschelein-Kleiner, "Microanalysis of Hydroxyquinones in Red Lakes," *Mikrochimica Acta* 6 (1967), 1080–1085; Masschelein-Kleiner, Nicole Znamenski-Festraet, and Luc Maes, "Les colorants des tapisseries tournaisiennes au xvᵉ siècle. Etude comparative de trois fragments de la Bataille de Roncevaux," *Bulletin de l'Institut Royal du Patrimoine Artistique* 10 (1967–1968), 126–140; Masschelein-Kleiner, Znamenski-Festraet, and Maes, "Etude technique de la tapisserie tournaisienne au xvᵉ siècle. Les colorants," *Bulletin de l'Institut Royal du Patrimoine Artistique* 11 (1969), 34–41; Masschelein-Kleiner and Maes, "Etude technique de la tapisserie tournaisienne aux xvᵉ et xviᵉ siècles. Les colorants," *Bulletin de l'Institut Royal du Patrimoine Artistique* 12 (1970), 269–279; Masschelein-Kleiner and Maes, "Etude technique de la tapisserie des Pays-Bas Méridionaux aux xvᵉ et xviᵉ siècles. Les colorants," *Bulletin del'Institut Royal du Patrimoine Artistique* 14 (1973–1974), 193–195; Masschelein-Kleiner and Maes, "Etude technique de la tapisserie des Pays-Bas Méridionaux. Les tapisseries anversoises des xviᵉ et xviiᵉ siècles. Les colorants," *Bulletin de l'Institut Royal du Patrimoine Artistique* 16 (1976–1977), 143–147; Masschelein-Kleiner, "Dyeing Techniques of Tapestries in the Southern Netherlands during the Fifteenth and Sixteenth Centuries," *Acts of the Tapestry Symposium*, November 1976, (San Francisco, 1979), 29–40; Masschelein-Kleiner, Maes, Marianne Geulette, and Maria Peeters-Keyaerts, "Etude technique de la tap-isserie des Pays-Bas Méridionaux. Les tapisseries bruxelloises au siècle de Rubens. Les colorants," *Bulletin de l'Institut Royal du Patrimoine Artistique* 18 (1980–1981), 183–187; Masschelein-Kleiner, Maes, and Jan Wouters, "Studie van de verfstoffen van de wandtapijten: De H. Paulus slaat Elymas met blindheid en De H. Petrus straft Ananias," *Wandtapijten uit de voormalig gentse Sint Pietersabdij. Geschiedenis, onderzoek en conservering* [exh. cat., Stad Gent-Byloke Museum] (Ghent, 1983), 29–34.

3. Masschelein-Kleiner, Maes, and Wouters 1983, 29–34; Jan Wouters, "High Performance Liquid Chromatography of Anthraquinones: Analysis of Plant and Insect Extracts and Dyed Textiles," *Studies in Conservation* 30 (1985), 119–128.

4. Jan Wouters, "Analyse des colorants des tapisseries brugeoises des xviᵉ et xviiᵉ siècles," *Bruges et la tapisserie*, ed. Stad Brugge and Ets Louis De Poortere S. A. (Bruges-Mouscron, 1987), 515–526.

5. Liliane Masschelein-Kleiner, "Le nettoyage des textiles anciens," *Bulletin de l'Institut Royal du Patrimoine Artistique* 13 (1971–1972), 215–221; Masschelein-Kleiner, "Le nettoyage des tapisseries: avantages et dangers," *Restauration et conservation des Tapisseries*, ed. Institut Français de Restauration des Objets d'Art (Paris, 1984), 44–50.

6. Liliane Masschelein-Kleiner and Juliette De boeck, "Contribution to the Study of the Conservation of Monumental Tapestries," ICOM *Committee for Conservation, Seventh Triennial Meeting* (Copenhagen, 1984), 84.9.33–84.9.37.

7. Juliette De boeck, Michelle De Bruecker, Chantal Carpentier, and Kathrijn Housiaux, "The Treatment of Two Sixteenth-Century Tapestries at the Institut Royal du Patrimoine Artistique," *The Conservation of Tapestries and Embroideries, Proceedings of Meetings at the Institut Royal du Patrimoine Artistique, Brussels, 1987*, ed. Getty Conservation Institute (Marina del Rey, Calif., 1989), 113–117, pls. 48–49.

8. Karen Finch, "Tapestries: Conservation and Original Design," *Conservation* 1989, 67–74; Ksynia Marko, "Two Case Histories: A Seventeenth-Century Antwerp Tapestry and an Eighteenth-Century English Soho Tapestry," *Conservation* 1989, 95–101.

NOBUKO KAJITANI

Conservation of Courtiers in a Rose Garden

A Fifteenth-Century Tapestry Series

In 1964, during an intended one-year visit to the United States from Japan, I met Joseph V. Columbus at the Textile Museum, Washington. My visit was arranged through Mary E. King and Junius B. Bird in order to do conservation work at Joseph Columbus' laboratory for a few days on a group of pre-Columbian textiles owned by my American hostess, Harriet Tidball of the Shuttle Craft Guild. On my second day at the museum, while I was busy stitching one of the textiles, Mr. Columbus interrupted me to say, to my surprise, "You have to stay here at least three months if you wish to learn how to take care of museum textiles." I followed his kind suggestion. My apprenticeship with him and James W. Rice continued for a year and seven months. This was a great accidental beginning for a textile conservator-to-be. I present this paper as a tribute to Mr. Columbus with my deepest gratitude for his initial guidance, which provided the foundation for my professional approach and development.

The fifteenth-century series of three tapestries known as the *Courtiers in a Rose Garden* has been exhibited at the Metropolitan Museum of Art since its acquisition in 1909 (figs. 1, 2, and 3).[1] All three tapestries depict elegant strolling courtiers and foliage of blossoming rose bushes superimposed on broad stripes of bold red, white, and green. The striking effect of the three contrasting design elements in the picture makes the series outstanding among the other medieval tapestries in our galleries, which are of a conventional pictorial genre. Constructed of wool, silk, and metallic yarns, the series is believed to have been woven in either France or the southern Netherlands in the mid-fifteenth century and represents one of the early phases in the history of tapestry making. Aside from the three tapestries in this series, only a few other extant fragments from this group are known.[2] These three tapestries, both individually and as a set, are beautiful, rare, and important works of art.

Adolfo S. Cavallo has generously allowed me to summarize his detailed entry for the *Courtiers in a Rose Garden* series from his catalogue of the medieval tapestry collection in the Metropolitan Museum of Art.[3]

The figures depicted on the tapestries are aristocratic personages. They are shown, however, without historical or narrative context and function simply as design elements on the tapestries.

The heraldic usage of the broad red, white, and green stripes can be compared to the wall hangings depicted in a miniature painting in Giovanni Boccaccio's De Casibus virorum illustrium,[4] *Bayerische*

fig. 16 (detail)

79

Staatsbibliothek, Munich, one of the few known parallels. The miniature painted by Jean Fouquet (c. 1420–c. 1480) illustrates a scene of the trial of the duc d'Alençon, which took place in a chamber of the château de Saint Georges at Vendôme in 1458. In it, Charles VII (1422–1461) of France presides in the center of the miniature, seated in front of a series of wall hangings that depict paired winged stags bearing the arms of France surrounded by stylized climbing roses against the background of broad red, white, and green stripes. Specialists have noted that the winged stag and the roses on the wall hangings, as well as the rose and iris flowers that are compartmentalized in the narrow border framing the Munich miniature, were among the motifs used as Charles VII's personal emblems. The three colors in the background, red, white, and green, have also been noted as his livery colors. These emblem motifs and livery colors could have been used in works of art commissioned by any one of the king's subjects as visual references to honor the king.

The livery colors of Charles VII and the striped-ground tapestries from the miniature indicate the possibility that the Courtiers in a Rose Garden *series may have been a part of a group of hangings containing some heraldic connotation. It is known that Charles VII favored blue, red, and white early in his reign—as had Charles V (1364–1380) and Charles VI (1380–1422) before him—but by 1437 he had chosen to use green in place of blue. Aside from this, however, there is no evidence to substantiate a claim that the* Courtiers in a Rose Garden *were woven for Charles VII either for his own use or as a gift to one of his subjects.*

Although the design of the series may have originated in France, the tapestries were probably woven in the southern Netherlands between 1450 and 1455.

The *Courtiers in a Rose Garden* series ranks among the great works of art from the medieval period. Representative and reflective of the period and place of manufacture, the series is unique, even among medieval tapestries, not only for its design

but also for its materials and technical components. The resulting manifold textures and subtle, well-balanced colorings create the indisputable visual impact of these tapestries.

Because of their beauty and rarity, these three tapestries have been on display at the museum, or in special exhibitions, virtually all the time since their acquisition. (One tapestry traveled to three exhibitions at five sites).[5] The Medieval Tapestry Hall, where the series has been exhibited, is located in the central section of the museum. The gallery, which has no windows or outside walls, is within the original museum building of 1880. The area was later connected to newer buildings on all sides to facilitate traffic flow to other

1. No. 09.137.1, with linen frame-borders, 1935 conservation work; warp 248 cm (98 in.), weft 315 cm (124 in.)
The Metropolitan Museum of Art, New York, Purchase, 1909, Rogers Fund

2. No. 09.137.2, with
linen frame-borders,
1935 conservation work;
warp 325 cm (128 in.), weft
289 cm (114 in.)

The Metropolitan Museum of Art,
New York, Purchase, 1909, Rogers
Fund

parts of the museum and was air-conditioned in 1982.

Despite our preservation efforts, it became evident that the tapestries needed radical conservation work, largely to correct the restoration work done at the turn of the century and in 1935.[6] In 1970 a proposal for conservation work on the *Courtiers in a Rose Garden* series was initiated by the department of textile conservation; the present conservation/preservation project began in 1979.[7] In consideration of future preservation within the context of the needs and conditions of the museum, textile conservators evaluated the intrinsic qualities of the tapestries, the positive and negative aspects of the fifty- to one-hundred-year-old conservation materials and techniques applied to them in the past, and the environmental conditions in which they were maintained during this period. The subsequent study of these underlying factors provided a basis on which to experiment first with techniques and materials, next to formulate our strategies for a long-term conservation/preservation program, and then to prepare step by step the fundamentals required for their treatment. The actual work on the tapestries finally began in March 1986.[8]

It was an honor to work on the *Courtiers in a Rose Garden* series, an opportunity that would occur only once in more than a century.[9]

The Materials and Technical Features of the Original Tapestries

It is conceivable that the three tapestries were originally woven as part of a larger set of an unknown number. At present, each tapestry is composed primarily of fragments of an original tapestry amended by reweavings and filler restorations to form a rectangular shape. Although no longer retaining their original dimensions, they have remarkably survived without having been separated as a result of the passage of time, historical events, varied uses, changes of ownership, and radical restorations.

At present, including restorations, each tapestry measures:[10]

09.137.1   height 3.15 m   width 2.48 m
09.137.2   height 2.89 m   width 3.25 m
09.137.3   height 3.79 m   width 2.64 m

The material components and construction features, as well as the state of material fatigue of the original *Courtiers in a Rose Garden* tapestry fragments described below, conform to the characteristics and conventions unique to the masterfully woven tapestries of the same period and provenance. (A discussion of past restorations will follow.) Because of the limited space allotted for this paper, a discussion of chronological occurrences of these features in the three tapestries compared with other tapestries is not included.

09.137.1

There are six original tapestry fragments (fig. 4). Five of the fragments are identifiable as being from a single tapestry; the material components and conditions in their junctures unmistakably match each other, revealing that they were originally woven as a single piece. A sixth small fragment, which had been cut to fill the missing lower right corner, does not match other juxtaposed fragments, indicating that it belonged elsewhere either as part of the same or one of the other tapestries in the series. Approximately five percent of this tapestry is composed of filler added during restoration. Approximately ten percent of the original tapestry fragments, namely dark brown, dark blue, and dark green wool and silk areas, have been rewoven.

09.137.2

There are seven original tapestry fragments (fig. 5). Five of the fragments are long vertical pieces that essentially separate the three figures in the picture. The piece on the far right has a sixth fragment appended to the lower edge. On the left half at the bottom is a long horizontal seventh matched fragment; on the right half is a large section of filler restoration. Another minor filler restoration area is located at a section along the top edge. Approximately three percent of this tapestry

3. No. 09.137.3, with linen frame-borders, 1935 conservation work; warp 264 cm (104 in.), weft 379 cm (143 in.)
The Metropolitan Museum of Art, New York, Purchase, 1909, Rogers Fund

is composed of filler restoration pieces.
Approximately twenty percent of the original tapestry fragments, namely dark
brown, dark blue, and dark green wool and
silk areas, have been rewoven.

09.137.3

There are five original tapestry fragments
(fig. 6), essentially divided into two vertical groups. The right-hand group is composed of three original fragments. The
left-hand group is composed of two original fragments with a fairly large angled
filler restoration area in the lower section
of the tapestry. The entire top edge has
been completely restored with filler
restoration. Except for the small piece at
the lower left, all the junctures of the five
original pieces unmistakably match each
other. Approximately twelve percent of
this tapestry is composed of filler restoration pieces. Approximately ten percent of

the original tapestry fragments, namely
dark brown, dark blue, and dark green
wool and silk areas, have been rewoven.

All three tapestries have the following
features in common:

- Viewed in their pictorial positions, the warps
  run horizontally in the width of the tapestry,
  and the wefts run vertically in its height.

- Various potential causes for the major damage or fragmentation can be conjectured.
  The top edges were probably fragmented by
  tearing as a result of the strain from hanging.
  All four sides have been cut, presumably to
  eliminate damaged or frayed edges and to fit
  the tapestries into smaller spaces. Some
  holes may have been caused by vermin.
  Fortunately, the tapestries have escaped
  destruction from vandalism.

- As all four sides have been cut, none of the
  original selvages and warp-end finishes
  remain. As a result, the tapestries' original
  dimensions cannot be deduced from their
  present state.

- Although the present edges of the tapestries
  appear to have been cut off, there are no
  traces of integrally woven borders at pictorially complete edges. The tapestries thus conform appropriately to the conventional bor-
  derless format found in other tapestries in
  this group.

- All three tapestries retain a soft, pliable
  hand, proof of past wetcleaning, which has
  removed the sturdy stiffness generally associated with unwashed, intact loom
  products.[11] The initial wetcleaning must
  have changed the original dimensions by a
  shrinkage of probably no more than two to
  five percent, possibly in different ratios for
  the warp and weft directions. This must
  have changed the proportions of the original
  composition.

The Wool Warp

The wool fibers for the warp yarn are
undyed, "white" in color, fairly coarse,
long, and shiny (fig. 7a). The fibers seem to
have been prepared fairly roughly for spinning and were rather tightly twisted into a
Z-spun single yarn. Then four Z-spun single yarns were again tightly twisted into
an S-plied yarn.[12] They were thus specifically prepared to be unstretchable, sturdy,
and strong for the purpose of supporting

the particularly vigorous tapestry-weaving process and for the eventual function of the piece as a wall hanging. The yarns are irregular in diameter as a result of spinning, which is compounded by plying and results in a subsequent weave that shows uneven ribs caused by the irregular warp (see, for example, figs. 9 and 12).

As of 1989, when they were approximately 530 years old, those warps that are still covered or protected by the interlacing wefts are in excellent condition. The warps that have been exposed by disintegrated wefts, or those at cut or broken edges, became weak and fuzzy as they untwisted and loosened over the years during wetcleaning and handling.

The Wool Weft

The wool weft yarns constitute roughly eighty-three percent of the tapestry. The fibers, which appear to be the same as the warp, were "white" when the yarns were spun and were subsequently dyed. The fibers for the majority of yarns were prepared fairly roughly for spinning, and the yarns were spun in an uneven diameter, tightly twisted into a Z-spun single yarn. In 09.137.1 and 09.137.3, the majority of wefts were made up of two Z-spun single yarns simply doubled without plying (fig. 8a), a characteristic more frequently found in tapestries of earlier periods. The random and spaced occurrence of convolution in the doubled yarns in the weave, which gives the appearance of plying, is probably not the result of intentional plying but rather of winding or unwinding the yarns from skeins, reels, and bobbins or butterflies during the course of handling and weaving. (Since plying is not an essential factor in yarn used for weft in nonfunctional wall hangings, it is conceivable that plying could have been omitted.) The differing tensions of each of the two irregularly and highly twisted weft yarns composing the doubled weft yarn created a minute and subtly irregular texture in these tapestries. In 09.137.2, the majority of wefts were made up of two Z-spun single yarns plied into S direction.[13] In each tapestry, in addition to the two major types already mentioned, weft yarns

5. No. 09.137.2, photographic composition of original fragments
Photo by the author

of several different compositions were also found at random locations: two S-spun yarns plied into Z direction; and in a freak exception, an S-spun single and a Z-spun single were doubled. In 09.137.3, there are areas woven with S-spun yarns quadrupled; they were used within monochrome hatchings that convey the appearance of fur trimmings (fig. 9a). The date of fabrication, the occurrence of irregularities in twist direction and diameter, and the characteristic of a high degree of twist suggest that the drop spindle or the spinning wheel without a flyer was used for spinning and plying.[14]

The uneven dyeing of the individual single yarns composing the doubled weft yarns used in tapestries 09.137.1 and 09.137.3 suggests that they may have been dyed in skeins while still single. The slight variations in color within the single yarns as well as among dye lots created the subtle color irregularities throughout the tapestries. In particular, within the monochrome stripes in the tricolor background, the irregular colorings softened the strongly contrasting, monotonous ren-

6. No. 09.137.3, photographic composition of original fragments
Photo by the author

dyes can be identified as those typical of the period, which monogenically produce red, blue, yellow, purplish red, and brown hues. Dyed singly or in sequential combination, the majority of dyed wool yarns are in fair but inferior condition when compared with the undyed off-white yarns, owing to the physically and chemically harsh dyeing treatment. The exception is the majority of wool yarns in brown hues attained by the use of rapidly oxidizing iron as a mordant. These yarns completely disintegrated long ago, presumably as early as the eighteenth century. The shadows and outlines of the designs where these brown-dyed yarns were used have mostly disappeared, so that today we perceive the pictorial image either without the brown or with rewoven brown possibly added in the eighteenth century. Fragile original brown yarns remain intact in a few areas where they were surrounded and thus supported by yarns in better condition.

The general condition of the wool fibers is fairly good considering that they are more than five hundred years old. Characteristically, the "fuzziness" that appeared on the surfaces during the initial weaving has been lost over the course of time, owing to oxidation that has caused the microscale cuticles of the wool fibers, as well as the ends of the fibers projecting from the spun yarns, to disintegrate and fall away.

The Silk Weft

The silk wefts constitute roughly ten percent of the weft. The silk filaments, which appear to be relatively coarse, were loosely spun—not reeled out—into a Z-twisted single yarn by drawing out a cluster of filaments probably from a loosened mass of cocoons. After the two Z-singles were loosely plied into S direction, the S-plied yarn was then doubled—without twisting—and used as a weft (see fig. 7b). Based on their present chromatic state, they were probably dyed light blue, blue-green, yellow, and pink and were used mostly to enhance the garments and rose leaves, their glossy effect competing with the glittering gilt metallic yarn. Even later, as the

dition that would have occurred had they been woven with the uniformly plied yarn produced by the industrialized methods of later periods.

The plied yarns used in tapestry 09.137.2 and in the minor areas of the other two tapestries (see fig. 8b)—the yellow color in the rose leaves—were dyed after plying, which is indicated by the identical coloring and streakings on the two single-yarn components plied together. The areas woven with plied yarns therefore rendered the picture with a flatter, two-dimensional effect.

An off-white color in the weft yarn can be presumed to be the only undyed, natural color. All other colors are dyed. The

metallic yarns tarnished, the silk yarns effectively maintained their sheen.

As the records and manner of reweaving testify, at the time of conservation in 1935 the silk wefts were apparently in fair condition, although to some extent they had already lost both color and strength. Since then, more than fifty years of exposure to the gallery environment have accelerated their deterioration, causing them to become brittle. Almost all the silk wefts still present in 1935 were nearly gone by the 1970s. On the obverse of the tapestries, every other warp had become bare; in their compactly woven weft-faced tapestry weave structure, every other weft, which interlaced over the higher alternate warps, had disintegrated, leaving several-millimeter lengths from the same weft underneath the lower alternate warps. The other alternate weft, which interlaced over the lower alternate warps and under the higher warps, remained unbroken, so the structure of the tapestry was, on the whole, held together by them as initially woven. In the 1950s, mending stitches were darned into the progressively deteriorating, bare-warp areas through to the straps or the lining. However, each time the tapestries were physically handled during the routine museum dismantling, rolling, unrolling, and hanging, the broken silk wefts fell out despite the presence of the mending stitches. Now the silk wefts can be found exclusively in the delicate lines of the picture held in place by the surrounding wool wefts in fair condition.

The Metallic Weft

The metallic wefts, whose golden glitter originally detailed the patterns of the courtiers' garments and highlighted the rose plants, constitute approximately seven percent of the weft. They are composed of cut strips of gilt silver sheet[15] closely wound in *S* direction around the core yarn of *S*-spun, single, yellow silk (see fig. 7c). One can speculate that the dyed yellow color of the core yarn was probably intended to enhance the effect of the gilt silver—a common practice with these metallic yarns. However, here the

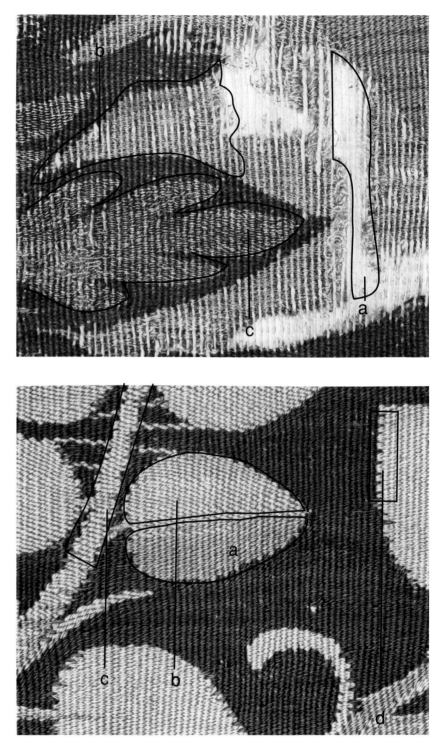

gilt silver strips were used singly as a weft, completely covering the core yarns without exposing the yellow silk. Each row was woven more sparsely than the wool or silk weft rows, as the inherent stiffness of the silver strips prevented

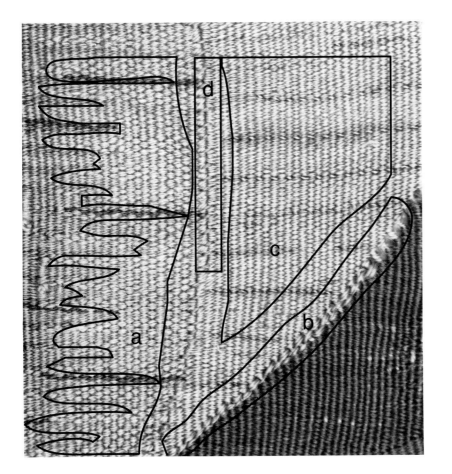

7. (opposite, above) Detail of a section in 09.137.3 (shown warp direction vertically with the top of the tapestry turned left), showing (a) warp, (b) silk weft, and (c) metallic weft
Photo by the author

8. (opposite, below) Detail of a section in 09.137.3 (shown warp direction vertically with the top of the tapestry turned left), showing (a) doubled single weft, (b) plied weft, (c) color junctures of slits, and (d) color junctures of grouped dovetailing
Photo by the author

9. (above) Detail of a section in 09.137.3 (shown warp direction vertically with the top of the tapestry turned left), showing (a) quadrupled weft, (b) non-straight weft, (c) alternate warps at slightly different levels, (d) slit-sewing stitches
Photo by the author

them from being interlaced closely and compactly in weft-faced plain weave, which requires considerable weft takeup. Although originally gilded, the silver content in the metallic strip has tarnished and now has a blackish appearance; strips with higher silver content, having excessively oxidized, have fallen off, leaving the bare core yarn. In such areas, the metallic remnants and the exposed silk core yarns are visible in a mottled "salt-and-pepper" effect. However tarnished, the remaining yarns are in fair condition and could probably maintain themselves for the next several hundred years.

The Dyes

Depending on the chemical composition of the dyes and dyeing auxiliary agents as well as environmental conditions, some of the originally achieved colors have been altered while others remain unchanged. The dyed yarns, also dependent on these

conditions, have either survived or disintegrated over this five-hundred-year period. The overall pictorial impact of the tapestries now appears considerably muted, since all shades of yellow, green, and red and the light blue, which cover most of the surface, have been reduced in value and altered in hue through fading by light, bleeding by washing, and/or the natural process of degradation of the dyes and fibers. The loss of the yellow hue in the green color used for the broad stripes, the garments, and the rose leaves—elements of great pictorial significance in these tapestries—has changed the color so that they appear a ruinous blue or greenish blue. Particularly unfortunate is the alteration of the dark green in the heraldic background stripes to a blue color. The colors that remain unfaded are shades of brown and medium-to-dark blue. The latter, which can also be found as a component in the green shades, has been enhanced by every wetcleaning, since the color is refreshed by washing. These arbitrary changes of shades have altered the color contrasts, reducing them in some areas where two faded colors are juxtaposed while increasing them in other areas where an unfaded and a faded color are juxtaposed. As a result, the original visual impact of the picture has inevitably been altered. The reverses of the tapestries still retain this striking impact, albeit in reversed image, in the range of potentially near-original colors that aid our estimate of the original renderings.

A number of different dyes and dyeing auxiliary agents were used to color the silk and wool fibers in these tapestries. In addition, the state of fibers/yarns, dye sources, auxiliary agents, water, pH (acidity to neutral to alkalinity), temperature, as well as procedures, technical methods, utensils, seasonal timing, and other factors each played a role in achieving the colors characteristic of tapestries with this provenance. Following the common practice in conservation work of attributing a dye source to a color in tapestries of this period and provenance, we first estimated the possible dyes used and then serially tested samples with reagents[16] and examined them under ultraviolet light in comparison to sample yarns, which we dyed using dyes we have collected as secure references. Further analyses on the identification of certain chemical classes in the dyes will be conducted when we have the opportunity.

In the *Courtiers in a Rose Garden* tapestries, four of the five principal hues of wool and silk yarns—red, reddish brown, yellow, and brown—were dyed from plant sources classified as mordant dyes using alum mordant to obtain a higher chroma, and iron mordant to obtain a lower chroma:

- Red hues: probably fresh root of madder (*Rubia tinctorum*).

- Reddish brown hues: dried woody tissue from the brazilwood family (*Caesalpinia* species).

- Yellow hues: fresh whole plant primarily of weld (*Reseda luteola*) and some other plants.

- Brown hues: various dried woody tissue and bark of trees and galls that contain tannins.

From the dye group of oxidizing dyes, probably only one plant was used.

- Blue hues: the whole plant of woad (*Isatis tinctoria*), which was first composted in order for the plant composites to break down while the dye remained. A chemical reduction was then applied for dyeing.

Some of the hues were produced independently and by sequentially dyeing and overdyeing different colors, such as yellow and blue to produce a green color.

In general, the fibers mordanted with alum are still in fair condition, whereas those mordanted with iron have disintegrated; the extent of disintegration has varied, depending on the amount of iron in the dye bath. This deterioration was probably evident as early as the eighteenth century for some yarns, while others may have remained intact as late as the twentieth century.

In the *Courtiers in a Rose Garden* tapestries, the following colors can be identified (see table opposite).

A brownish cast to the fibers, which gradually appeared as a result of the inevitable process of oxidation and soiling since its previous wetcleaning in 1935, was removed by our wetcleaning process dur-ing the present conservation project. In the future, as the fibers oxidize, the brownish cast will slowly return.

Structural and Technical Features

The weave structure of the *Courtiers in a Rose Garden* tapestries can be described as tapestry weave or weft-faced weave with discontinuous wefts, with the junctures of the discontinuous weft, interworked in slits, dovetailing, grouped dovetailing, and double-interlocking.[17] Junctures of slits (see fig. 8c) were utilized not only to change colors but also to demarcate the pictorial elements: slits composed of one or two wefts, which created dotlike shadows, were compositely aligned to appear as lines (fig. 10a). The demarcation lines created three-dimensionality in what would otherwise have been flat monochrome blocks. Dovetailing (fig. 10b), and grouped dovetailing (see fig. 8d), which were utilized in place of long slits for the narrow horizontal lines in the picture, effected short hatchinglike shadows. Double interlockings (fig. 10c), which have technical restrictions, created an uninterrupted plain weave surface on the obverse and were used exclusively in the courtiers' faces to achieve the delicate details. The wefts were interlaced basically at a right angle to the warp except for the areas that required curvilinear emphasis in the picture. Here, they were woven in a non-straight or curved alignment, effectively but subtly contributing to the creation of a three-dimensionality in the picture (see figs. 9b, 11a). The discreet but effective use of nonstraight wefts, combined with the use of straight lines and selective application to particular details of the picture, created the delineation of the design elements unique to these tapestries. In addition, the weft yarns liberally filled the broad colored stripes, section by section, occasionally creating lazy lines of up to ten centimeters. These yarns are laid in straight alignment in the warp direction or at a slight diagonal (fig. 11b) in both directions. They are located at the random distance of a weaver's arm's reach, at approximately ninety-centimeter intervals. These random methods of filling the

Color	Dye/Mordant	Comments
red	madder/alum	Approximately three shades can be identified. At present, the darker the shade, the closer it is to the original, despite the loss of yellowish hue; the lighter the shade, the farther from the original, due to fading. The darkest shade was used predominantly in the background stripes.
bluish red	madder/alum with indigo	There are approximately four shades from very dark to light. Nearly all of the red colors used in the pictorial elements were woven in this red shade to contrast with the above-described red used in the background stripes.
brownish red	brazilwood/alum	On the obverse, this color, which was used for the garments, has completely faded to faint beige, indiscernible as a red color.
purplish red	madder/alum with indigo	One shade can be identified. This red color was used in necklaces and stockings.
yellow	weld/alum	The number of originally intended colors cannot be identified, as their fading is drastic. One or two shades are recognizable today in the rose leaves and some parts of the garments.
brown	tannin/alum tannin/iron	Very light brown may or may not have been dyed. Reddish and yellowish browns in light, medium, and dark shades—used in dresses and hats and all shadows and outlines—can be recognized. Practically all the browns dyed with iron mordant have disintegrated, leaving little trace.
blue	indigo	Approximately three light, medium, and dark blue shades can be identified. Unintentional streaking between the shades of light and medium blue predominates in silk. The blue colors were used in garments and hats.
near black	indigo/tannin/iron	A very dark bluish black, found in the stockings, has completely disintegrated.
green	indigo/weld/alum	Approximately three light, medium, and dark green colors, varying from yellowish to bluish, can be identified. As the yellow dye has faded, all the green colors are now much more blue than originally intended. They were used in the background stripes, garments, and leaves and stems of the rose plants.

monochrome background also break up the flat homogeneous effect common to most of the more neatly produced tapestries of later periods.

The men's and women's plain garments were woven in either wool or wool and silk, whereas decorated garments were rendered in wool, silk, and metallic yarn; their fur trimmings and linings were woven in wool. The hats and headdresses were woven in wool with some highlighting in silk; the stockings and shoes were woven in wool yarns. Jewelry and a variety of accessory objects were also woven in metallic and silk yarns delicately delineated with brown wool yarns.

The rose blossoms are white where they appear against the red and green background stripes and are red where depicted against the white background stripes. The inner parts of the roses were woven in two shades of pink wool yarn, the center containing the stamen in metallic yarn, and the sepals in metallic and silk yarns. The roots, stalks, and leaves were also woven with silk, metallic, and wool yarns.

The three-dimensionality of the pictorial elements, or contrasting brightness and shadow, was effectively created by the use of hatchings, an established convention in tapestry weaving that employs a sawtooth counterchange of up to seven different colors, one after another. The hatching effects cause the figures and gnarled trunks of the rosebushes to appear so profoundly three-dimensional that they effectively contrast with the flat, monochromatic, broad-stripe background.

Sporadically, in all the tapestries, the level of alternate warps is perceptibly higher than the other warps (see fig. 9c), probably indicating the use of a vertical loom. Judging from the manner and technical details, one can speculate that the weaving may have begun at the right edges and ended at the left edges, with the weavers facing the reverse side. This is consistent with the presence of double-interlocked weft junctures and the systematic manner in which the unwoven weft yarns were carried along the reverse according to the progression of the weaving. As yarns were a precious commodity in that period, the unwoven weft yarns were very sparingly left loose on the reverse of the tapestries.

The longer slits were closed by sewing in overcast stitches, with the same wool yarn used for the weft (see fig. 9d). This was possibly done on the loom as a length of slit occurred during the process of weaving. There is no evidence of post-weaving techniques such as embroidery, painting, or appliqué.

Because of the spinning methods—done fairly unevenly without well carding the fleece—the yarn-makeup of doubling, rather than plying, and dyeing singles, which were all done without mechanical perfection, the weft yarns in the tapestries

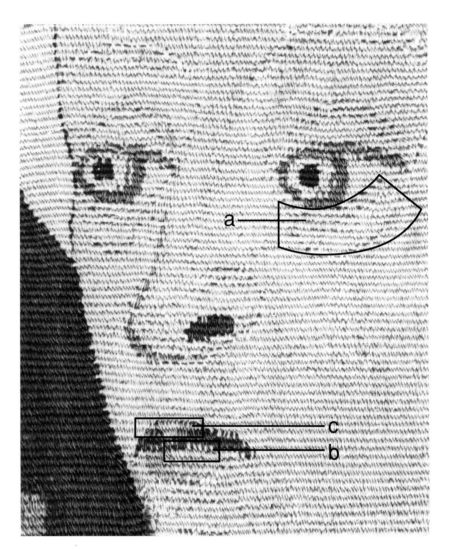

are uneven, thick and thin, highly twisted and less twisted, with streaked colors. The uneven makeup and streaked colors of the doubled weft yarns, while interlacing softly but compactly in tapestry weave over the unevenly prepared warp yarns, create manifold textures and subtle colorings. As a result, the *Courtiers in a Rose Garden* tapestries exhibit color renderings unique to the group. (Upon close examination, one recognizes that each of the three tapestries was woven somewhat differently or possibly by different hands.) In the early stages of the development of tapestry-making, the same person probably served as weaver and designer, or else worked within the smaller unit of artisans not yet divided into separate trades. Sheepherding, spinning, harvesting the cultivated and wild dye plants, and dye-

10. Detail of 09.137.3 (shown warp direction vertically with the top of the tapestry turned left), showing (a) composite slits line, (b) color junctures of dovetailing, and (c) color junctures of double-interlocking
Photo by the author

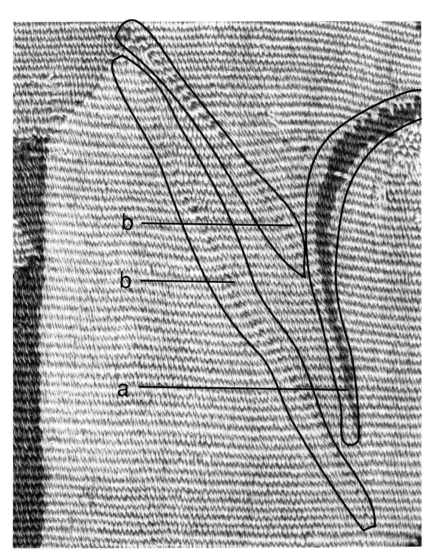

11. Detail of 09.137.3
(shown warp direction vertically with the top of the
tapestry turned left), showing (a) non-straight weft and
(b) diagonal lazy line
Photo by the author

ing might also have been done within the
same group. It is possible that the *Courtiers
in a Rose Garden* tapestries were woven in
such a setting. The weavers seem to have
well understood how to create the details of
the pictures with the available coarse yarns
that were dyed in a limited number of colors—each weft yarn, woven line by line,
contributes to the delicacy of the depiction.
The aesthetic virtuosity of these tapestries
was thus largely due to the artisans who
used the most simple materials, weaving
the most basic structure while understanding how the nature of these materials, given
the technical limitations of the time, could
contribute to pictorial effect. Such craftsmanship must have been nurtured over a
long period; these works could not have
been done on a whim.

History, Material, and Technical Features
of Past Restoration Work

At present, the pictures in the tapestries
are complete as a result of three probable
stages of radical reweaving undertaken in
the past: the first, probably in the eighteenth century, incorporated uniformly
spun yarns dyed with natural dyes; in the
second stage, about the beginning of the
twentieth century and before the museum's acquisition, machine-spun yarns
dyed with early synthetic dyes were used.
The third, in 1935, after the museum's
acquisition, saw the addition of framelike
linen cloth borders. Prior to the museum's
acquisition of the tapestries in 1909, the
restoration was exclusively reweaving;
none of the missing areas was patched
with fragments from alien tapestries, as is
often done with this type of early tapestry.
Each stage of restoration, the evaluation
of which follows, reflects the perspective
on aesthetics and technical character of
that particular period.

The Eighteenth-Century Restoration

The extensive reweaving that was done
using wool yarns dyed with natural dyes
can be distinguished from other restorations that used wool yarns dyed with synthetic dyes. These reweaving yarns are of
hairlike wool fiber, evenly prepared, spun,
and plied (three loosely S-spun yarns combined) and evenly dyed (probably after the
yarns were prepared).

Judging from the type of spinning and
dyeing and the manner of reweaving, this
restoration was probably done in the eighteenth century. The reweaving appears to
have been done when eighteenth-century
tapestries, realistically depicted, were in
vogue, whereas fifteenth-century tapestries, deemed *primitive* and *used*, were
not yet regarded as high art forms.
Although relatively orderly, the craftsmanship of this first reweaving can in no
way be considered a serious effort. It was
done casually and without sensitivity in
comparison to the artistic quality and
craftsmanship of the original as well as
the later reweavings.

Having withstood possibly two hundred years of exposure, the fibers from the first restoration are still in good condition. The colors, which were uniformly distributed on the yarn, still retain the unfaded colors. Having common dye sources, the colors in the original tapestries and these reweaving yarns are harmonious, even if most of the latter are more intense and do not reproduce exactly the same hues as the original colors.

However acceptable the quality of the materials used, the technical caliber of this reweaving is inferior. The reweaving did not follow the exact details of the originals, and the selected colors do not match the original ones. The use of tannin/iron-dyed brown yarns seems to have been avoided, with dark blue used instead. The overall effect and the pictorial sensibility of the tapestry have, therefore, been greatly altered by this reweaving.

Some corrections are essential. For example, to enhance their three-dimensionality, the demarcation lines between the various juxtaposed design elements in closely graduated or identical colors were originally indicated by the use of slits and non-straight wefts. In this restoration, these design elements—for example, the sleeve, the body of a jacket, and its fur trimming—were rewoven with the same color wefts in straight alignment and without slits; as a result they appear as one contiguous flat plane (fig. 12). In the majority of large rewoven areas, mostly concentrated in the garments, the colors are not only unlike the original colors but also fill the approximated spaces without delicately following the original orderly hatching pattern. Although one might be inclined to remove these unsightly restorations, with discipline, most of the reweavings have been left intact during the present conservation project because of their relative color harmony.

The Turn-of-the-Century Restoration

With the second restoration, which was completed before the Metropolitan Museum of Art acquired the tapestries, they seem to have gained renewed respect as works of art; the reweaving was done meticulously with skilled craftsmanship and an unobjectionable, if not refined, understanding of the detail in the pictorial renderings. In all three tapestries, the areas rewoven are extensive and include all of the filler restoration pieces, all of the junctures that assembled the original fifteenth-century fragments, and details in the original fragments.

This reweaving is distinguished by the use of undyed cotton yarn for the warp, and for the weft, a thinner, brownish metallic yarn, a highly degummed and thus extremely shiny silk yarn, and a finely spun worsted wool yarn. The reweaving was technically neat and evenly executed. Still in good condition are the undyed cotton warp yarns (two Z-spun single yarns S-plied, then the three S-plied yarns were replied in the Z direction), as well as the wool weft yarns (several different kinds of relatively hairy fibers, Z-spun single yarns S-plied, in different colors combined to produce a mottled, mixed color effect). Unfortunately the colors of the weft, dyed with the type of synthetic dyes then newly invented and manufactured, have drastically faded after only eighty years.

12. Detail of fig. 6. Dark brown shadows, which were originally possibly woven showing different pictorial planes according to their locations, have been rewoven as one plane, using one color and without using composite slits line
Photo by the author

No concern was apparently focused on the lightfastness of these dyes, which were considered sophisticated at the time they came into use. With constant exposure to gallery lights accelerating the problem, none of the dyes have retained their original colors; for example, a madder-simulated red has faded to light wine-red, losing its original yellow hue; tannin/iron-simulated dark brown has faded to orange, purple, or pink; indigo-simulated dark blue and medium blue have faded to gray; and indigo/weld-simulated dark green has faded to light yellow-green. For the excessively light colors, the rewoven areas stand out conspicuously as blotches, stripes, and bands, substantially reducing the aesthetic impact of the original tapestry designs. During the present conservation project, these reweavings, though otherwise technically excellent, have been mostly replaced with new reweaving, with the exception of the large reconstructed fillers.

The approximately eighty-year-old silk reweaving yarns (two S-twisted yarns Z-plied, then two Z-plied yarns combined without plying) were made of much finer filaments and more lustrously degummed than the original silk yarns. They have already deteriorated more rapidly than the original silk yarns now more than five hundred years old. In addition, all the colors of the silk weft yarns, which are now a uniform shiny cream color, have probably completely faded from their originally dyed colors.

The alloy strips used in the metallic yarn (a strip of an alloy wound around in S direction over the three-strand yellow silk yarn core, each in a slight S-twist) are still sturdy but have tarnished to a copper-brown color, which gives the rewoven areas an unattractive brownish salt-and-pepper effect. Because their diameter is about half the size of the original metallic yarn, they were used in combination with a brown and a khaki silk yarn to thicken them. In our present conservation program, depending on the surrounding areas to be restored, these metallic yarns are selectively replaced with a new cotton reweaving yarn in the color of the original metallic yarn.

The 1935 Restoration, after the Museum's Acquisition

At the time of the third restoration, the tapestries were wetcleaned.[18] Then the wooden picture frames (fig. 13), on which the tapestries had been mounted prior to the museum's acquisition, were replaced with picture-frame-like borders of 5 centimeters wide, undyed linen basket-weave cloth (see figs. 1, 2, and 3), probably conforming to the aesthetic taste of that period. The tapestry was then prepared for hanging. On the reverse, a series of medium-weight (30-cm-wide) cotton cloth straps for support were sewn with a silk buttonhole thread and spaced approximately 40 centimeters apart (fig. 14). A full lining of lightweight linen cloth was then attached over the straps (fig. 15) with cotton sewing thread. To provide allowance, the lining was vertically shirred at 30-centimeter intervals and stitched to the straps. A jute webbing was then sewn with heavy-duty linen thread along the top edge through the lining and the tapestry. For wall installation, the webbing was tacked onto a wooden slat, which was in turn hung by wires and S-hooks from picture hangers. (Shortly after the conservation work it was recorded that the tapestries were fumigated in a cyanogen gas chamber in the museum in order to prevent insect attack.)[19]

The hanging system long employed by the museum has proved to best serve our needs. The conservation materials used to devise this system in 1935 provided us with an opportunity for a useful evaluation after more than fifty years of use. It is presumed that these materials were selected from the available and industrially mass-produced twentieth-century merchandise manufactured for general use, not for museum-oriented longevity or long-term use. After only fifty years, some of these conservation materials have barely endured exposure to the gallery environment. By the early 1970s, the three bast-fiber materials—linen lining, linen border cloth, and jute webbing—and the silk sewing threads had deteriorated and, by the 1980s, were shredding (see fig. 15). Linens processed by today's economically oriented methods cannot be trusted out-

13. No. 09.137.2, in wooden
picture frame placed before
the museum's acquisition in
1909
The Metropolitan Museum of Art,
New York, Purchase, 1909, Rogers
Fund

right to be a long-lasting conservation material. In contrast, the eighteenth- and early nineteenth-century linens used on other tapestries are still in good condition; the longevity of these pre-industrial-period linens, processed by traditional methods, is being confirmed. Jute fiber webbing, with its inherent high lignin content that is commonly known to deteriorate rapidly, was traditionally manufactured for short-life products such as grain sacks and packaging twines, never for long-term uses such as hanging tapestries in a museum. Research on the background of materials can lead to an understanding that conventions of the time are generally based on valid reasoning. In contrast to the bast-fiber cloth used for lining, borders, and webbing, the cotton cloth used for straps has survived in fair condition.

The 1956 Attachment of the Zipper Security System

The lower parts of the tapestries swayed in the breeze while hanging in the gallery. In 1956, in order to prevent the flapping caused by uncontrollable air movements, sets of zippers were devised to stabilize the tapestries on the walls.[20] A continuous length of heavy-duty metal zipper was cut to the lengths of the two sides and bottom edge of each tapestry; one side of each zipper was sewn onto the appropriate edge of the tapestry, and the other side was tacked onto the wall at predetermined positions. After the webbing at the top was tacked onto the wall, the sliders were inserted to connect the three zippers, thereby stabilizing the tapestry on the wall. The system secured the tapestries but also served to

14. No. 09.137.2, reverse of the tapestry. The strapping and lining attached in 1935 being removed in 1989
Photo by the author

15. No. 09.137.2, reverse of the tapestry. The 1989 condition of the deteriorated linen lining attached in 1935. Note shirring on the lining
Photo by the author

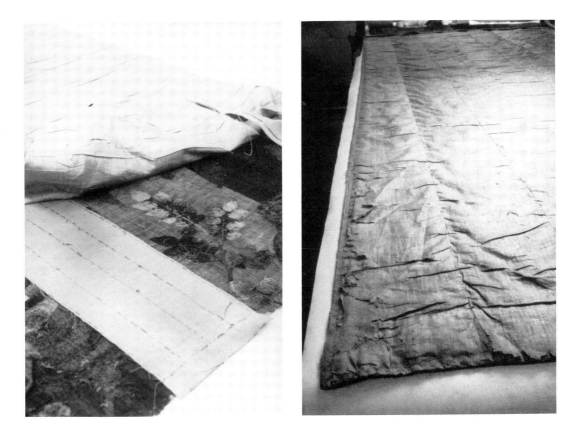

prevent their removal from the gallery walls, even to storerooms, for seventeen years. (No other tapestries in the collection were large enough to hang over and conceal the zipper/frame on the wall.) This system was phased out in the mid-1970s, ironically increasing our chances to handle the tapestries.

Recent Maintenance Program

The current system of conservation maintenance of the medieval tapestries went into effect in 1966. The department of textile conservation maintains a file for each tapestry in the *Courtiers in a Rose Garden* series, which contains: a record sheet logged with the activities relevant to the tapestry; a four-page technical analysis sheet; a dye analysis record; photocopies of photographs color-marked for past and present restorations, notable damages, and other features of the tapestry; recommended criteria for environmental and

physical conditions for exhibitions, storage, and transport; photographs and slides of the tapestry in full view and detail; conservation records; and interdepartmental memos and correspondence. Records of activities before the inception of this system in 1966 are incomplete.

In the late 1960s it was observed that the original silk wefts, which were still in fair condition at the time of the 1935 restoration, had deteriorated to the point of falling off the tapestries each time they were handled. The fifty-year-old linen frame-borders and the lining also began to fall apart on the wall, partly because of continuous exhibition in the gallery and partly because of inherent material fatigue. It was recommended that the tapestries no longer be physically moved. (The loan request for the tapestries to travel for the first time to Paris in 1973 for the special exhibition, *Masterpieces of Tapestry*, thus had to be declined.) Nevertheless, they were twice handled to accommodate repainting the walls and changing their installation. In 1981 the tapestry with large silk areas (09.137.2)—the only tapestry that traveled to five outside exhibition sites—had to be placed in storage to await conservation work.

Ongoing Conservation Project, 1987 to the Present

The goal of the present conservation work is to improve the visual, physical, and chemical condition of the three tapestries in the series for their long-term preservation. Their pictorial impact will be corrected, as far as is possible, to their original state, given their present condition. To this end, it was decided that the tapestries were to be finished by showing all the edges to their maximum; the 1935 frame-borders (see figs. 1, 2, and 3) should be removed and not replaced, as the conventional format of tapestries of this period and provenance is believed to have been without borders.

Our objectives are:

- Analysis and assessment of the present state of the original and the restorations.

- Formulation of a strategy for long-term preservation, which includes selection of materials with potential longevity, appropriate techniques of conservation laboratory work, and provision of an optimum environment.

- Essentially, the laboratory work includes wetcleaning, correction and refinement of the past reweavings, particularly the faded yarn in the turn-of-the-century restoration, and the renewal of a hanging system.

The material components of the original *Courtiers in a Rose Garden* tapestries have already survived more than five hundred years. How much longer can they survive? It is the goal of our conservation work to preserve these tapestries for another five hundred years in an appropriate manner that is not detrimental to the original material components and that does not make use of materials like the 1935 linings and short-lived, turn-of-the-century dyes, which deteriorate faster than those originally used. The number of hours required for the present conservation work, if the work is done efficiently, should not be a consideration. Throughout

the conservation, we aim to provide optimum physical, chemical, and mechanical conditions for preservation of the original fragments and past reweavings as well as conservation materials to be used in the tapestries. All these materials must be long-lasting, of high quality, and well suited to the intended treatment in terms of their aesthetic and functional features; we strive to execute all technical work with appropriate aesthetic judgment and utmost skill to produce an unobtrusive result. The guidelines are based on exclusive technical and material selections for the *Courtiers in a Rose Garden* tapestries, as well as on generalized practices "tested" in our museum over more than one hundred years of maintenance. For these tapestries in particular, we are fortunate to have observed the performance of techniques and materials used in past conservation work under various environmental conditions, and have been able to determine how these efforts have aided or damaged them. Our perpetual query in this context is the unpredictable longevity of the conservation materials and colorants we use.

Although no generalizations can be made about the longevity of conservation materials, some guidelines are evident. We have observed, for example, that virtually all silks produced since the early twentieth century that were used in textiles, tapestries, and conservation materials have deteriorated more rapidly than eighteenth-century silks or any other fibers. Consequently, instead of silk, we have chosen cotton yarns, threads, and cloths, and for lining and webbing, cotton and synthetic fiber threads and cloths. Wool seems to have a fair degree of longevity.

Five conservators who have experience with medieval tapestry conservation are engaged in the project.[21] The tapestry (09.137.2) depicting a lady and two gentlemen, which has been in storage for several years, was the first tapestry to undergo treatment. The conservation work began in March 1987 and was completed in February 1989 (fig. 16). The second tapestry (09.137.3) is currently under treatment, and the third (09.137.1) is scheduled to be completed in 1995.

Several factors contributed to the two major conservation decisions to undertake wetcleaning and reweaving of the tapestries.

• Regarding wetcleaning: since the present conservation work provides a rare opportunity for the tapestries to be relieved of straps and linings and even most of the reweaving for the first time since the 1935 restoration, it was decided to wetclean them. Provided that the tapestries will be better cared for in the future than in the past, they will not have another opportunity to be wetcleaned for the next several hundred years, or for as long as they are preserved. Since previous wetcleaning has removed the initial intact characteristics of the original hand, texture, and dimensions, our wetcleaning will not further alter these aspects. It was not difficult to predict that the remaining portions of the original silk wefts, which were barely held in the tapestry, would not last long. But it was also not difficult to predict their loss to a degree in our wetcleaning solution. It took many years of consideration, up until the last moment, to reach the conclusion that the tapestries should be wetcleaned despite the anticipated loss.

• Regarding reweaving: we are now fortunately able to replace some of the original disintegrating yarns—such as the rose leaves in yellow silk—and the old reweavings by merely tracing or following them, without having to guess or invent most of the pictorial content. It was therefore decided to correct the tapestries' pictorial effect by reweaving, the method used a number of times in the past on this series.

To begin conservation work, the tapestry was first vacuum-cleaned. The fifty-year-old 1935 conservation materials were removed: the disintegrating jute webbing, linen lining, and linen framing borders; the cotton straps in fair condition; the cotton and linen sewing threads in fair condition; and the silk sewing threads, which had already left dye crockings on the neighboring fabrics and were so deteriorated that they broke when we touched them.

The tapestry, intact with its reweavings and soiling but free of conservation materials, was then photographed. Intended largely to function as a reference during our reweaving process, slides were taken of identical areas from the obverse and the reverse, in a grid of approximately 20 centimeters by 30 centimeters rectangles. The grid was marked with threads to facilitate matching photography after treatment.

The tapestry was then prepared for wetcleaning. Some reweavings, which during wetcleaning would protect the original tapestry, were untouched. Others were removed if the original yarns subsequently exposed by the removal of covering restoration could withstand the wetcleaning. All colors/dyes from both original and restoration yarns were tested for wetfastness. To protect the weakened areas throughout the wetcleaning procedures, cotton tulle nets were sewn locally over the obverse and the reverse.

Directly before wetcleaning,[22] dyefastness was retested, using solutions of the exact composition and temperature as those to be used for washing. Our indoor wetcleaning facility consists of an inclined washing floor with a trough at one end. The tapestry was laid on stainless-steel support screens. Monitoring with a surface pH meter, wetcleaning was performed with an unlimited supply of temperature-controlled demineralized water of pH 6.5 and a temperature of 23°C, enhanced by the use of an anionic detergent made of saturated fatty acids as a primary component, with a pH between 7.5–8. Enough workers were available to accomplish the entire operation in approximately six hours. The pH of the tapestry was initially 4.4 and finally at 5.7. The ensuing drying was done in the same location, first using towels to absorb much of the moisture, then allowing the tapestry to dry at room temperature, aided by moderate air circulation.

The drying was concluded in twenty-four hours.

The tapestry was then moved onto a worktable for further acclimatization and the simultaneous removal of reweavings insofar as this was feasible. The original tapestry without reweavings should have been photographed again, area by area, matching the previous photography, but this was not possible because the tapestry was no longer in a state to withstand the extra manipulation.

To prepare the tapestry for the reweaving operation on a set of reweaving rollers (fig. 17),[23] the tapestry was opened out on the worktable with its reverse side facing up. Lengths of cotton cloth were sewn onto both warp ends of the tapestry as extensions, then the tapestry was rolled from each end—with the aluminum tube rollers laid parallel to the wefts—beginning with the extension cloths. The tapestry's obverse side was then placed face up by moving one of the rollers over to the other. The pairs of rollers, designed to be placed parallel to each other at opposite ends of a worktable with a reweaving space reserved between them and the worktable, was then placed into a pair of holder-stands. There are three reasons for placement of the worktable between the rollers: (1) it considerably reduces the amount of the rolled portions of the tapestry, and therefore the diameter of the rolled rollers around which the conservators' arms must move and work constantly; (2) it readily enables the conservators to refer to the larger sections of the tapestry visible while working on a minute area often under 3x magnification (although the exposed portion is generally covered up); and (3) the roller holders were devised so that the rollers can be readily removed and placed on the worktable to allow study of the reverse of the tapestry.

In physical appearance, however hard we try to simulate the texture of the original yarn, modern reweaving materials will never be able to recreate the identical texture of the original tapestry. The smooth and shiny surface of the original tapestry yarns, owing to the deterioration of the fibers with the passage of time, cannot be simulated by new yarn. In its physical

17. Tapestry restoration roller
Photo by the author

strength, the type of yarn used for weaving a tapestry, in which a yarn is simply carried between alternate warps opened out as sheds, cannot be used for reweaving because of the repeated friction borne by penetrating in and out between warps. Our selection of the reweaving yarn was, therefore, based primarily on its smoothness and strength to withstand friction. Given the fact that tapestries of this size are viewed from a certain distance, their visual impact is most significantly affected by the colors in the reweaving yarn; its textural differences, by contrast, are less discernible.

For the areas originally woven of wool, a wool reweaving yarn (2 *Z*-spun yarns plied into *S*) was used;[24] since its twist is higher than that of the original yarn, the rewoven surface does not resemble the texture of the original, but it achieves an appearance and function that are acceptable and accommodates various requirements for the restored tapestry. For areas that were originally silk, a mercerized cotton yarn (2 *Z*-spun yarns plied into *S*) was used;[25] despite its having a higher twist than that of the original, the longevity of cotton will better serve the tapestries, as modern silks are highly degummed, appear excessively more lustrous than the original fifteenth-century silks, and degrade faster than any other fibers. For

the areas with the original metallic yarn, the same mercerized cotton yarn was used. In both cases, two or three different colors were combined to make the reweaving appear closer to the original silk or metallic yarn. Where the strength of the original warps did not tolerate our reweaving process, new warps, using the same yarn as the weft, were inserted.

In selecting colors, we simulated the present color effects—mostly faded—as they are seen on the obverse of the tapestry, rather than the colors as they appear on the reverse, which more or less retain the original values. To simulate the color effects in the overall worn-out tapestry in its existing condition, reweaving wefts were woven in sparsely, not compactly, occasionally exposing the warps. As a result, when seen from a typical tapestry-viewing distance, the rewoven areas chromatically blend well with the original areas that are more than five hundred years old. At close range, however, the rewoven areas appear variegated and sparser than the tapestry as originally woven. For example, the dark brown colors used extensively to render all demarcations and shadows of the design elements have mostly disintegrated. Where they do remain, however, they have retained their original dark hues. In our treatment, a range of lighter and variegated brown colors compatible with the surrounding areas was used to replace these so that the newly restored dark brown reweavings would not stand out too strongly in contrast to the overall faded tapestry.

The wool reweaving yarns were dyed in the laboratory, using bichrome complex metal dyes.[26] The lightfastness of the yarns was spot tested with a fadeometer.[27] In summary, the yarns dyed with 1.5 percent to 3 percent dyes per weight of yarn were found to be equal to AATCC's lightfastness classes "4, fairly good" to "5, good": the accelerated light exposure in the test can be interpreted as equivalent to 100 lux lighting in the gallery for three hundred years. (In the gallery the lighting is actually controlled to the maximum of 80 lux.) This could be interpreted to mean that in the coming years the original colors in the tapestries could potentially fade more than those of our reweaving yarns. However, with the *Courtiers in a Rose Garden* tapestries, the rate of past fading on the fifteenth-century yarns has unfortunately reached a point at which further fading will probably not be evident.

In the first phase, while continuously characterizing the nature of the technical features pertaining to the areas to be rewoven, the work was begun and categorically proceeded so that the conservators could become accustomed to the tapestry. The deteriorated rose leaves originally woven with yellow silk and scattered throughout the tapestry were rewoven first. Shifting from a leaf in one branch to a leaf in another, each conservator rewove different branches in order to mix and scatter the variations in the individual styles of reweaving. After the leaves were mostly rewoven, each conservator, with increasing confidence, took charge of refining old reweavings in each figure of the courtiers. To assist in their understanding of the tapestry, conservators from time to time studied paintings of the period in our galleries, slide library, and art reference library.

Our discussions focused on the criteria for judging how and to what extent to restore the various areas of deterioration and damage, which distort the design and harm the tapestries as wall-hanging pictures. Experiments for practical solutions to these problems were devised. The decision to retain some of the eighteenth-century reweaving, which is materially acceptable but pictorially unacceptable, was a difficult and delicate compromise. Although we were tempted to correct this, we disciplined ourselves to leave most of this type of reweaving intact. In restored areas where there were no traces of original yarns, such as in the shoes, all the crowded reweavings from different periods were left untouched. Because the impact of color is so important in appreciating tapestries, as the reweaving progressed, some of the turn-of-the-century faded restoration yarns, though skillfully rewoven and still in good condition, were removed and corrected if they were deemed pictorially, chromatically, structurally, or functionally obtrusive, or did not blend well with the surrounding areas. The improvement of the effect achieved by this work, as each faded restoration weft was gradually substituted by our new yarn, cannot be overstated.

After reweaving was completed, the tapestry's irregular side edges were sewn onto strips of cotton fabric, and then these edges were folded a minimum of 3 millimeters, with the cotton fabric creating straight edge lines, and securely stitched. Then we followed our predecessors' hanging system using improved materials: cotton strap and lining fabrics prewashed for shrinkage adjustment, cotton or synthetic fiber webbings, Velcro™ tapes, security tabs, poplar wood sealed with polyurethane resin for a hanging slat, and copper wire and steel hooks for hanging. The functional longevity of these conservation materials can only be properly evaluated in thirty to fifty years.

The conservation work on 09.137.2 took approximately fifteen months, approximately 4,500 hours. The completed tapestry (fig. 16) was hung in the Medieval Tapestry Hall. The climate is controlled to maintain a temperature of 23°C, with a relative humidity of 45 percent, an air velocity of less than 3 meters per minute, a maximum level of ambient illumination at 80 lux, and an ultraviolet-ray emission level at less than 75 lumens over the tapestry. These factors, as well as the visitor traffic patterns in the museum, impel us to keep daily monitoring as a vital part of our conservation program.

As the conservators of the *Courtiers in a Rose Garden* tapestries for a very short time period of its long past and future history, we hope our daily efforts, no matter how minute, will contribute to their preservation for centuries to come.

NOTES

I am most grateful to the following teacher-colleagues: Stanley Bulbach, Adolfo Cavallo, Bette Hochberg, and Angela Lakwete for their unreserved discussion on specific topics while preparing the article; in the Metropolitan Museum, William Wixom and Timothy Husband, department of medieval art and The Cloisters, for their longtime support for my study and conservation projects for the museum's precious medieval textiles and tapestries; Robert Koestler, department of objects conservation, for elemental analysis; Alexander Mikhailovich, formerly of the photo studio, for photography; departmental staff members Kathrin Colburn, Tina Kane, Elena Phipps, Midori Sato, Florica Zaharia, and former staff member Sophie Hawkes for their dedicated conservation work on the *Courtiers in a Rose Garden* tapestries and for reading and refining this manuscript.

1. Accession no. 09.137.1 (two ladies and three gentlemen), Rogers Fund. Accession no. 09.137.2 (a lady and two gentlemen), Rogers Fund. Accession no. 09.137.3 (four ladies and four gentlemen), Rogers Fund. The following Metropolitan Museum of Art publications discuss the series: "Fifteenth Century Tapestries," *Metropolitan Museum of Art Bulletin* 4 (New York, 1909), 149–152, pl. A (photographs of 09.137.1, .2, and .3); Joseph Breck and Meyric Rogers, *The Pierpont Morgan Wing*, 2nd ed. (New York, 1929), 130–131, fig. 42 (photograph of 09.137.3); James J. Rorimer, *Medieval Tapestries: A Picture Book* (New York, 1947), fig. 5 (photograph of 09.137.2); James J. Rorimer and William H. Forsyth, "The Medieval Galleries," *Metropolitan Museum of Art Bulletin*, NS., 12 (New York, 1954), 135, illus. 137 (photograph of 09.137.2).

2. The Metropolitan Museum of Art owns another tapestry fragment that is of the same type as the *Courtiers in a Rose Garden*: 41.400.231 (a gentleman), 1.98 m x .97 m, Gift of George Blumenthal.

3. Adolfo Salvatore Cavallo, *Medieval Tapestries in The Metropolitan Museum of Art* (New York, 1992).

4. Paul Durrieu, *Le Boccace de Munich* (Munich, 1909), pl. I, 55.

5. The three exhibitions at five other museums were: *Arts of the Middle Ages*, Museum of Fine Arts, Boston, 1940; *2000 Years of Tapestry Weaving*, Wadsworth Atheneum, Hartford, and Baltimore Museum of Art, Maryland, 1951–1952; *The Middle Ages: Treasures from The Cloisters and The Metropolitan Museum of Art*, Los Angeles County Museum of Art and Art Institute of Chicago, 1970.

6. Many museum staff members have participated in the preservation efforts of the *Courtiers in a Rose Garden* series over the years. Curatorial staff who have overseen these efforts include: the late James Rorimer, former director; the late Margaret Freeman, curator; William Forsyth, Margaret Frazer, Carmen Gomez-Moreno, former curators; Barbara Boehm, Charles Little, William Wixom, present curators. Conservation staff who have worked on the series include: Kate Lefferts, former conservator; the late Helen Burke, the late Matilda Sullivan, former textile restorers; Alice Blohm, Sophie Hawkes, Jane Hutchins, Fuyuko Matsubara, Karen Meyerhoff, and Won Yee Ng, former textile conservators; Kathrin Colburn, Tina Kane, Elena Phipps, Midori Sato, and Florica Zaharia, present textile conservators. Installation has depended on the efforts of Charles Anello, former upholsterer; Martin Fleischer and Vincent Juliano, former technicians; Thomas Vinton, present technician; as well as riggers, electricians, and building engineers.

7. In the memo dated 13 February 1979, Carmen Gomez-Moreno, curator, department of medieval art, requested Nobuko Kajitani, textile conservator, department of textile conservation, to plan the conservation project.

8. Through the efforts of Philippe de Montebello, director, and William D. Wixom, chairman, the department of medieval art and The Cloisters, the museum allocated funds for the project during the fiscal years 1987–1988, 1988–1989, and partially 1989–1990. For the fiscal years 1989–1990 and 1990–1991 by the arrangement of Emily K. Rafferty, vice president for development, a generous grant from the Louis and Virginia Clemente Foundation partially funded the project.

9. For the general approach and conservation/preservation principles implemented in this project, see the three articles by the present author: "Technical Notes" (accompanying Vera Ostoia's "Two Riddles of The Queen of Sheba"), *Metropolitan Museum Journal* 56, nos. 1 and 2 (New York, 1973), 97–103; "The Preservation of Medieval Tapestries," *Acts of the Tapestry Symposium, November 1976* (San Francisco, 1979), 45–63; and "Conservation Maintenance of Tapestries at The Metropolitan Museum of Art, 1984," *The Conservation of Tapestries and Embroideries* (Marina del Rey, Calif., 1989), 53–66.

10. For an analysis of technical features of each tapestry, see appendix, this essay. Corrections or changes may be made in the future as the current conservation work progresses and when detailed study and work have been completed.

11. Although wetcleaning might have been done a few times in the past, only the last wetcleaning on the museum premises in 1935 was recorded. See note 18.

12. See Liliane Masschelein-Kleiner, "Study and Treatment of Tapestries at the Institut Royal du Patrimoine Artistique," elsewhere in this volume.

13. No. 09.137.2 may be considered to have been woven later than 09.137.1 and 09.137.3.

14. Bette Hochberg, *Handspinner's Handbook* (Santa Cruz, Calif., 1980); *Handspindles* (Santa Cruz, Calif., 1980).

15. A sample of a "cut strip of gilt silver sheet" of the metallic weft yarn from 09.137.3, removed by the department of textile conservation, was exam-

ined by Robert Koestler, department of objects conservation. An examination of its morphology by scanning electron microscopy-energy dispersive x-ray spectrometry showed the composition to be mostly silver (>75%, by weight), with a low percentage of gold (approximately 10%, by weight) and a very low percentage of copper (approximately 2%, by weight).

16. Judith Hofenk-de Graaff, "A Simple Method for the Identification of Indigo," *Studies in Conservation* 19 (London, 1974), 54–55; Liliane Masschelein-Kleiner, "Dyeing Techniques of Tapestries in the Southern Netherlands during the Fifteenth and Sixteenth Centuries," *Acts of the Tapestry Symposium*, November 1976 (San Francisco, 1979), 29–40; Helmut Schweppe, "Identification of Dyes in Historic Textile Materials," *Historic Textile and Paper Materials: Conservation and Characterization*, Advances in Chemistry Series 212, ed. H. Needles and S. Zeronian (Washington, 1986), 153–174.

17. Irene Emery, *Primary Structures of Fabrics* (Washington, 1966), 73–90; Kajitani 1973.

18. Information in the museum's catalogue department includes the following:

In June, 1935, these tapestries were stretched, washed with an ivory[sic] soap emulsion and thoroughly rinsed. Then they were relined and loose threads picked up. The restorers were the Curator and the Museum upholsterers. J.J.R[orimer]. MG These tapestries have been treated in the cyanogen gas chamber as a precaution against moths. (P. S. Harris, June 5th, 1937 LC)

This wetcleaning session can be assessed as similar to the one performed on another tapestry in 1966, described and discussed in Kajitani 1989, 57.

19. See note 18.

20. Conservation requisition by William Forsyth, curator, department of medieval art, dated 30 April 1956. The work was completed by Helen Burke, textile restorer, conservation department, on 14 December 1956.

21. The author, department of textile conservation, formulated and supervised the project. The departmental staff assisted in general laboratory work. For reweaving at the initial phase of the first tapestry, 09.137.2, Sophie Hawkes, Tina Kane, and Midori Sato were engaged. Sophie Hawkes and Midori Sato

completed the first tapestry. Sato and Florica Zaharia are engaged in working on the two remaining in the project, 09.137.3, then 09.137.1.

22. Kajitani 1979 and 1989. James W. Rice, "Principles of Textile Conservation Science, No. I—General Chemical and Physical Structural Features of the Natural Textile Fibers," *Textile Museum Journal* I–I (Washington, 1962), 47–51; "Principles of Textile Conservation Science, No. IV—The Conservation of Historic Textile Colorants," *Textile Museum Journal* I–2 (Washington, 1963), 55–61; "Principles of Textile Conservation Science, No. V—The Characteristics of Soils and Stains Encountered on Historic Textiles," *Textile Museum Journal* I–3 (Washington, 1964), 8–17; "Principles of Textile Conservation Science, No. VI—The Wonders of Water in Wetcleaning," *Textile Museum Journal* II–I (Washington, 1966a), 15–22; "Principles of Textile Conservation Science, No. VII—Characteristics of Detergents for Cleaning Historic Textiles," *Textile Museum Journal* II–I (Washington, 1966b), 23–37; "Principles of Textile Conservation Science, No. IX—How Humidity May Affect Rug, Tapestry, and Other Textile Collections," *Textile Museum Journal* II–3 (Washington, 1968), 53–60.

23. Henry Wolcott, Jr., conservation department, designed the versatile device, which was made in the museum's carpentry shop in 1968. Wallace and Melvina McGarr, Norwood Loom Company, Michigan, arranged to have four ratchets, pawls, and handles cast.

24. The yarn was custom produced to our specification by Allen Fannin: 100% natural white virgin wool, 2/25 worsted, spun 15 tpi Z in each single, 12 tpi S in the ply.

25. The mercerized cotton yarn was purchased from the DMC Corporation, six strand Art. 117, an embroidery-thread series.

26. The dyes used were Irgalan series, Ciba-Geigy Limited. For dyeing, an Ahiba sample dyeing machine, Texomat, was used.

27. The test was conducted in 1985 by Won Yee Ng, department of textile conservation (supervised by E. René de la Rie, then of the department of painting conservation), which owns the Atlas C:35 fadeometer, following the AATCC Test Method 16E–1982, "Color Fastness to Light: Water-Cooled Xenon-Arc Lamp, Continuous Light."

APPENDIX

09.137.1 Two Ladies and Three Gentlemen

Dimensions: Height 3.10 m Width 2.51 m.

Materials:
Warp
Wool, 4 *Z*-spun yarns, *S*-plied; undyed; 14 warps per 2.5 cm.

Weft
Wool, 2 *Z*-spun yarns doubled. Several shades each of light pink to red, light to dark green, yellow, light to dark blue, brown; two shades of red brown; undyed. 50–60 wool wefts per 2.5 cm.

Silk, 2 *Z*-spun yarns *S*-plied; doubled. Light blue; light green; yellow. 90 silk wefts per 2.5 cm.

Metallic, gilt silver cut strip wound around yellow silk core, *S*-wound. 80 metallic wefts per 2.5 cm.

09.137.2 A Lady and Two Gentlemen

Dimensions: Height 3.33 m Width 3.84 m.

Materials:
Warp
Wool, 4 *Z*-spun yarns, *S*-plied; undyed; 14 warps per 2.5 cm.

Weft
Wool, 2 *Z*-spun yarns, *S*-plied. Several shades each of light pink to red, light to dark green, yellow, light to dark blue, brown; two shades of red brown; undyed. 50–60 wool wefts per 2.5 cm.

Silk, 2 *S*-spun yarns, *Z*-plied; light blue; light green; yellow. 90 silk wefts per 2.5 cm.

Metallic, gilt silver cut strip wound around yellow silk core, *S*-wound. 80 metallic wefts per 2.5 cm.

09.137.3 Four Ladies and Four Gentlemen

Dimensions: Height 3.81 m Width 2.67 m.

Materials:
Warp
Wool, 4 *Z*-spun yarns; *S*-plied; undyed; 14 warps per 2.5 cm.

Weft
Wool, 2 *Z*-spun yarns doubled. Several shades each of light pink to red, light to dark green, yellow, light to dark blue, brown; two shades of red brown; undyed. 50–60 wool wefts per 2.5 cm.

Silk, 2 *S*-spun yarns, *Z*-plied; light blue; light green; yellow; pink. 90 silk wefts per 2.5 cm.

Metallic, gilt silver cut strip wound around yellow silk core, *S*-wound. 80 metallic wefts per 2.5 cm.

CAROL BIER

Knots and Bolts

Design and Technology in the Caucasus

In the largest sense, Oriental rugs represent both the social history and manufacturing traditions of their particular cultures and are related to the human needs, economies, and ecological constraints of those societies. Each textile or fragment represents a complex set of human interactions between user and viewer, implying a social response, and between user and maker, sometimes resulting from economic transactions among buyer and seller, lender, merchant, and trader. Suppliers of raw materials and market superintendents or commissioners for fair trade and quality control may also have been involved. The quality and appearance of any given textile results from the contemporaneous conjunction of such factors as taste, knowledge, technology, social traditions, aesthetic preference, fashion, political and economic circumstances, household organization, availability of raw materials, and ecology of surroundings. In short, every textile ever produced, from oversize carpets to the tiniest scrap of a fragment, is the product of its own environment, made and used in response to a particular set of historical circumstances.

Oriental carpets have long been appreciated in Europe and America.[1] Rich colors and attractive designs, as well as lush pile and renowned durability, have given them a well-deserved reputation as beautiful and useful floor coverings. As handmade products of distant lands, their complicated patterns also evoke the romance of luxury and the East of long ago. The familiar Oriental carpets that have graced the parlors and drawing rooms of American middle-class homes are, for the most part, commercially produced and marketed.

Less well known are the tribal and ethnographic weavings of peoples of the Near East (figs. 1, 2, 4, 5, and 8–12). Although such rugs have a long history, they have become known in the West only recently.[2] The many varieties of flatweaves, as opposed to pile carpets, are the Near Eastern structural equivalent of European tapestries. Yet flatweaves (rugs without pile) from the Near East are distinctly different from European structural counterparts, probably due primarily to particular circumstances of production and their cultural context. Near Eastern flatweaves were generally woven by and for the people who used them rather than for commercial sale. Worn and well used, and only rarely available in the markets and bazaars of Cairo, Istanbul, Tblisi, and Bokhara, those that survive today were produced in the nineteenth and early twentieth centuries by rural sedentary and nomadic population groups in Anatolia, Persia, the Caucasus, and Central Asia, which today fall within the present borders of Turkey, Iran, and the southern republics of the former Soviet Union.

fig. 13b

Cultural Contexts

Many peoples settled in the mountainous regions between the Black and Caspian seas, known as the Caucasus. Some migrated from elsewhere and were halted by the barrier of the great mountains. Others passed through the area as merchants, sometimes leaving an imprint of their

1a. (left, above) Embroidery with sunburst design, silk on cotton; balanced plain weave ground with long flat stitch. Central Caucasus, eighteenth century; warp 117 cm (46 in.), weft 66 cm (26 in.)

1b. (left, below) Detail
The Textile Museum 2.6, acquired by George Hewitt Myers in 1915

2a. (right, above) Pile carpet with embroidery pattern in sunburst design, wool; plain weave ground with cut supplementary weft, symmetrical knot. Central Caucasus, eighteenth century; warp 531 cm (209 in.), weft 231 cm (91 in.)

2b. (right, below) Detail
The Textile Museum R36.2.12, acquired by George Hewitt Myers

3. Pile carpet with dragon design, wool; plain weave ground with cut supplementary weft, symmetrical knot. Central Caucasus, eighteenth century; warp 495 cm (195 in.), weft 236 cm (93 in.)
The Textile Museum R36.1.1, acquired by George Hewitt Myers in 1916

in which design and structure are more closely linked.[3]

Flatweaves have been produced in all areas of the rug-weaving world. Generally they are less costly and less time-consuming to make than rugs with knotted pile. Heavy and rugged, flatwoven textiles serve many purposes.[4] They are used as covers for walls, floors, bedding, and low tables or are placed over the hearth. Some are hung in doorways or in front of recessed areas that serve as closets and cupboards. Others are containers for storage and transport; still others are saddle cloths or animal blankets. In some areas, cradles are made by slinging a flatweave between strong wooden poles.

Pile Carpets from the Caucasus

Pile carpets represent an amalgamation of different design traditions. Between the Black and Caspian seas, south of the great Caucasus mountains, magnificent rugs were produced for humble use in towns and villages during the second half of the nineteenth century. Rugs from the Caucasus reached a peak of appreciation in the West at the turn of the century, when they became widely known for their bright colors and bold designs. These rugs reflect regional design traditions drawn from diverse sources. Beginning in the nineteenth century, Caucasian rugs were woven primarily for commercial purposes and for export. They probably represent the most distinctive design tradition of all rug-producing areas in the world.

The oldest-known rugs from the Caucasus are called "dragon" rugs (fig. 3), many of which were preserved in early Turkish mosques.[5] In contrast to more recent traditions of rug manufacture in the Caucasus, these are considerably larger than the commercial rugs of the nineteenth century. Although they share certain structural features and an array of color with rugs from the Karabagh region (in particular the "sunburst" group), they show consistent use of a warp on two levels (often referred to as "depressed").

Historically, dragon carpets date from a time when the Safavid Empire extended

own regional traditions in the arts. The richness of patterns in Caucasian textile arts is, in part, the result of the comings and goings of peoples from east and west, north and south.

Caucasian embroideries (fig. 1) and flatweaves are decidedly less well known than pile weavings in regions beyond the Caucasus. Produced as a domestic art, they were destined for home use and local commerce. Their bright colors and bold patterns also reflect ethnic and regional diversity. Where similar patterns occur in commercially produced rugs that are hand knotted (fig. 2), it is likely that they were copied from embroideries and flatweaves northwest into southern regions of the Caucasus. At the turn of the seventeenth century, Shah Abbas actively supported economic development throughout his realm. Commercial looms were established and supported in Kirman, Isfahan, Kashan, and Tabriz; he may also have been instrumental in establishing rug weaving in the Caucasus as a commercial activity. Certainly the width of dragon carpets required broad beams for their production, suggesting the need for substantial capital. Their stock designs, though complex, also hint at commercial production.

Three other design elements in Caucasian pile weavings are related to the stylization of dragons and secondary motifs included in the patterns of dragon rugs: blossoms in profile (sometimes referred to as palmettes), medallions based on two-dimensional geometric constructions, and sunbursts, a variant blossom form viewed from above (sometimes referred to as rosettes).

Flowers are the greatest single source of design inspiration in Oriental carpets. Rich varieties of natural forms are endlessly played with in creating graphic designs dependent on color, outline, and principles of symmetry. Floral forms, too, many to enumerate, proliferate in all textile arts of the Caucasus.

Within the layout of pairs of dragons and phoenixes in dragon carpets, stylized blossoms are most often presented in profile. The distinct arrangement of individual blossoms, with an identifiable top and bottom, sometimes lends an axial orientation to the carpet. Petals and base are displayed symmetrically on either side of a vertical axis. Similar blossoms occur as secondary motifs in carpets with sunburst designs and serve as individual pattern units in the central field of carpets with infinite repeats, arbitrarily terminated by surrounding borders. Sometimes these are disposed in a staggered alignment of blossoms offset in rows, creating a cellular appearance.

A favorite floral design in Caucasian weavings is the sunburst (figs. 1 and 2). It shows biaxial symmetry, with composite petals radiating from a central point. The geometric stylization of the flower is based on a primary orthogonal axis, with a

4a. Flatweave (kilim), wool; balanced plain weave ground with supplementary discontinuous weft, slit tapestry. Eastern Caucasus, nineteenth/twentieth century; warp 260 cm (102.25 in.), weft 137 cm (54.4 in.)

4b. Detail
The Textile Museum 1989.9.1. Gift of Charles Grant Ellis from estate of Arthur Arwine

5a. Construction: balanced plain weave.

5b. (below) Construction: warp-faced plain weave.

5c. (right) Construction: weft-faced plain weave (Emery 1980, figs. 85-87)

secondary orthogonal axis rotated forty-five degrees. The resulting floral rosette has a quadripartite division.

Squares, diamonds, hexagons, octagons, and star formations are also basic to the design of Oriental carpets. Like the blossoms in Caucasian weavings, these elements are playfully arranged and disposed. Very often, what at first glance appear to be simple geometric forms are, when viewed more carefully, seen to be effective geometric stylizations of buds and blossoms.

Rugs with dragons, blossoms, and sunbursts, as well as medallions, were produced in several regions south of the Caucasus Mountains. Carpets with dragon designs share stylistic and technical fea-tures suggesting production within a restricted geographic area. Their similarity in palette and structure to later products from the Karabagh region suggests manufacture there,[6] despite the fact that they were always referred to in the early rug trade as "Kuba," after the name of a commercial city in the eastern Caucasus. Sunburst designs also appear exclusively in rugs attributed to Karabagh, whereas blossoms in profile are more characteristic of rugs from eastern regions of the Caucasus, usually referred to as Shirvan and Daghestan. Medallion designs appear in rugs produced in all areas, but are more prevalent in products of tribal nomadic groups from the arid regions to the south. As in blossom and sunburst carpets, principles of symmetry are important in establishing the repertoire of visual images for medallion designs.

Near Eastern Flatweaves

In contrast to pile weaves, the design and weaving of flatweaves of the Caucasus are inseparably related. Near Eastern flatweaves represent many different textile structures, offering almost infinite possibilities for design. They often have a foundation in plain weave (figs. 1 and 4); that is, the simple interlacing sequence (over one, under one) of two sets of elements, warp (vertical) and weft (horizontal).[7] Plain

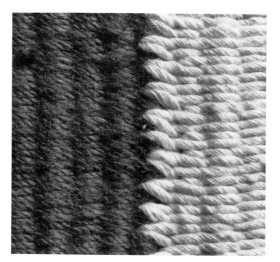

weave may be balanced (fig. 5a), warp-faced (fig. 5b), or weft-faced (fig. 5c). Traditional designs and patterns in Near Eastern flatweaves indicate an appreciation of a direct relationship between design and the process of weaving.

In weaving, the simplest design is a stripe or band produced by introducing different colors to the warp or weft, depending on whether the fabric is warp- or weft-faced. Horizontal bands across the fabric width result from changes in the weft colors carried from selvage to selvage in a weft-faced weave. Easier to weave, but initially more time consuming, is the setting up of striped warps, which in a warp-faced weave creates vertical stripes throughout the length of the fabric. More complex patterns (fig. 6) are made by the juxtaposition of color by means of discontinuous wefts (wefts not running through the full width of the fabric from selvage to selvage). This yields a generic structure often referred to as tapestry. The interface of color may be accomplished through various structural combinations: slit tapestry (discontinuous wefts return by wrapping around contiguous warps, fig. 7a); dovetailed tapestry (wefts return by wrapping around the same warp, one above the other, fig. 7b); interlocked tapestry or double-interlocked tapestry (wefts return

6. (left) Flatweave (kilim), detail, wool; weft-faced plain weave with discontinuous weft, slit tapestry. Eastern Caucasus, late nineteenth/twentieth century; warp 363 cm (143 in.), weft 167 cm (66 in.)
The Textile Museum 1989.10.65 (formerly L1978.5.75). Bequest of Arthur D. Jenkins

7a. Construction: weft-faced plain weave with discontinuous weft, slit tapestry

7b. Construction: weft-faced plain weave with discontinuous weft, dovetailed tapestry

7c. Construction: balanced plain weave with discontinuous weft, double-interlocked tapestry
(Emery 1980, figs. 93, 97, 103)

8a. (opposite, above) Flatweave (kilim), detail, wool; weft-faced plain weave with discontinuous weft and with outlining weft used to approximate a diagonal line, slit tapestry. Northern Persia, late nineteenth/twentieth century; warp 300 cm (118 in.), weft 170 cm (67 in.)
The Textile Museum 1989.10.91, (formerly L1978.5.105). Bequest of Arthur D. Jenkins

8b. (opposite, below) Flatweave (kilim), detail, wool; weft-faced plain weave with discontinuous weft and outlining weft used to emphasize structural characteristics, slit tapestry. Southeastern Anatolia, twentieth century; warp 375 cm (148 in.), weft 153 cm (60 in.)
The Textile Museum 1989.10.72 (formerly L1978.5.83). Bequest of Arthur D. Jenkins

by wrapping around each other, on the reverse of the fabric, fig. 7c). Double-interlocked tapestry with plain weave is indigenous to several cultural pockets in the Middle East, for example, in Afghanistan and central Iran among the Bakhtiyari people. This unusual structure may perhaps be related to the more

famous double-interlocked twill shawls produced in Kashmir that influenced European fashion and patterns for weaving.[8] Another method for designing tapestry with discontinuous weft is the introduction of an outlining weft. This may be used to approximate a diagonal line (fig. 8a), otherwise virtually unobtainable due to the inherent rectilinearity of weaving resulting from successive forward movements of the weft over and under alternate warps. An outlining weft may also be used to emphasize inherent structural characteristics of discontinuous weft tapestry (fig. 8b).

The use of supplementary wefts offers other design possibilities. In the Near East, two of the most popular techniques, which are sometimes combined, are called soumak and cicim. Soumak (figs. 9a and 9b) is supplementary weft patterning with a forward movement followed by a backward movement in the same shed. In effect, each weft is wrapped around successive groups of warps. This creates a system of diagonally aligned progressive structural elements, which may be countered to enhance the visual effect of the design. Cicim (figs. 10a and 10b) is supplementary weft patterning with forward and backward movements of the weft in different sheds, creating a series of progressive horizontal structural elements that may be placed in vertical alignment. Owing to the technical features of soumak and cicim, the designs created by each technique have different characteristics. Soumak patterning (fig. 9a) lends itself admirably to the strength of diagonal lines, whereas cicim (fig. 10a) permits the construction of diagonals as well as both horizontal and vertical lines. In contrast, slit tapestry (fig. 7a) forces a stepped approach to the creation of a diagonal line and precludes any possibility for long vertical lines in order to maintain the structural integrity of the fabric; dovetailed tapestry (fig. 11) lends itself more readily to approximate diagonal lines.

Extant flatweaves from the Caucasus demonstrate that weavers were cognizant of the design potential of each weaving technique. Their exploitation of the relationship between design and the process

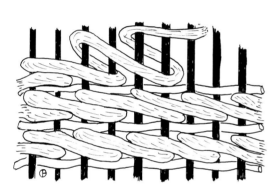

of weaving is evident in the resultant fabric structure.

Other means of patterning, familiar elsewhere, are less well known or nonexistent in flatweaves of the Caucasus. Complementary weft or weft substitution, known among Moroccan weavings and flatweaves attributed to the Baluch peoples of Iran and Afghanistan, for example, is absent among the wide varieties of woven structures documented in the Caucasus. The use of complementary warps (warp-floats or warp substitution), however, is present in narrow strips that represent local traditions spanning the Caucasus, northern Iran, and Afghanistan. This type of strip weaving is locally referred to as *jajim*, not to be confused with the supplementary weft patterning called cicim (in Turkish, *c* is pronounced like *j*).[9]

Senneh kilims (fig. 12) present a contrasting relationship between weaving and design. Extremely fine kilims with tiny repeat patterns are attributed to a region of Kurdistan in western Iran, in and around the town of Senneh. These kilims, all in slit-tapestry weave, are distinguished from other Near Eastern flatweave traditions in several ways. Whereas most flatweaves in the Near East derive from tribal and nomadic contexts and display a preference for geometric patterns that adhere to the technological parameters of weaving, the kilims of Senneh are unique in the curvilinearity of their designs. Curved lines are achieved through the use of eccentric wefts, filling in areas of design in a manner contrary to the normal rectilinear progression of weaving by sheds. The floral motifs and curving lines nearly tran-

11. Flatweave, wool; weft-faced plain weave with discontinuous weft, dovetailed tapestry. Caucasus, twentieth century; warp 317.5 cm (125 in.), weft 146 cm (57.5 in.), excl. fringe
Collection of James D. Burns (TM loan L1989.8.1)

12a. (right, above) Flatweave (kilim), wool; weft-faced plain weave with discontinuous weft, slit tapestry. Iran (Senneh), nineteenth century; warp 183 cm (72 in.), weft 118 cm (46.5 in.)

12b. (right, below) Detail
The Textile Museum 1989.10.45 (formerly L1978.5.54). Bequest of Arthur D. Jenkins

scend the inherently orthogonal interlacing of woven form by means of eccentric wefts as well as much finer yarn dimensions.

Senneh kilims are not the product of a nomadic environment; their curvilinear designs reflect urban artistic traditions, and the patterns relate more closely to commercially woven textiles and pile carpets.[10] According to current scholarship, this refined local flatweave tradition derives from Safavid court styles. Senneh was the capital of the Kurdish governors of Ardalan after the fall of the Safavid dynasty in the mid-eighteenth century. Production of these weavings may reflect

the artistic patronage and strength of local leaders.[11]

Design and Technology

Design in woven textiles is a function of interaction among structure, technique, and pattern. Structure is inherent as physical evidence in the fabric itself; technique is inferred and defined by the known processes of fabrication; pattern is created by manipulating the technical process to form the structures. Pattern may rely on the interaction of colors with structures as determined by techniques. This interaction of elements in three dimensions to create what is visually perceived as two-dimensional design distinguishes the textile arts from all others. The inherent structure of fabric is critical to the perception of design and pattern.

Precise descriptive vocabulary is required for an understanding of the basic role that structure plays in the formation of pattern. The strongest proponent for careful descriptive structural analysis and the development of standardized terminology today in the field of Near Eastern flatweaves is John Wertime, based on the initial work of Irene Emery at the Textile Museum in the 1960s.[12]

In pile weaving, tapestry techniques, and embroidery, the density of design units is determined by several factors: yarn dimensions (diameters of warp, weft, and supplementary elements); yarn construction and density, tightness of weave, and structure of weave (primary foundation); and the presence of secondary structures. Appearance is also affected by viewing distance. For pile rugs, knot density is expressed as knots per square linear unit of measurement. Knot density is further determined specifically by structural features such as the number of ground wefts between each row of knots; the type of knot (whether it is wrapped on a single warp, on double warps, or on double pairs of warps); whether each knot is symmetrical (sometimes called Turkish or Ghiordes knot); or asymmetrical (sometimes called Persian or Senneh knot); and whether the warps remain on a single level or are depressed, which is dependent on the tension of the weft. Depressed warps create a thicker fabric in which the knots have a much greater density per square unit of measure.[13] The increased density allows much greater flexibility in design, primarily because of greater possibilities for approximating visual curvilinear lines.

This potential for enhanced two-dimensional design, directly related to three-dimensional structural characteristics of pile weaving, was used to great advantage in Persian court carpets and in Indian court and commercial products strongly reliant upon Persian influence. Although these are structural considerations, they strongly affect not only the physical character of the weave itself and the design but also the visual perception of color, not unlike resolution on a computer screen.

In order to achieve a semblance of perfect symmetry in two dimensions, all elements in the three-dimensional structure of weaving that contribute to formation of the design must be of uniform dimension (warp, weft, and supplementary elements). This requires not only careful planning but also control over construction of the yarns. One way to judge the degree of planning at the design stage, prior to execution at the loom, is to notice if a particular carpet has identical horizontal and vertical knot counts throughout its field.

On seeing the nearly square Pazyryk carpet at the Hermitage Museum in St. Petersburg, which dates from the fifth-fourth century B.C.,[14] one has to admire the almost equilateral configuration of the designs, readable both horizontally and vertically. More frequently such designs are compressed along one axis. This characteristic is most evident in the borders of carpets where repeating motifs form a pattern that can be read vertically along the sides and horizontally at top and bottom. It is an indication of concern, careful planning, and quality control when side borders, top and bottom borders, and "corner solutions" display identical scale and proportion in the representation of design elements.

The weaver plays with geometry by alternating color, including juxtaposing dark and light in reciprocal arrangements and interspersing forms as well as varying the size of medallions. Unlike the painter with a brush, the weaver designs by manipulating yarns so that patterns are often integral to the structure of the fabric. This is particularly true of flatweaves, in both slit and dovetailed tapestry and in counted-thread embroidery. The wrapping and cutting of supplementary wefts in rug

13a. Embroidery, silk on cotton; balanced plain weave ground with cross stitch. Central Caucasus, eighteenth century; warp 150 cm (59 in.), weft 120 cm (47 in.).

13b. Detail
The Textile Museum 2.18, acquired by George Hewitt Myers in 1952

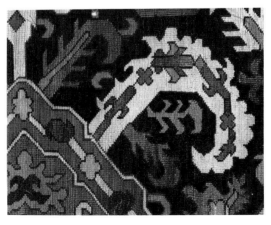

weaving are less tied to evident technological structure because of the length of pile and its modular dot matrix. Arrows, chevrons, crosses, hooks, and double-curving *S*-shapes lend a sense of intricate complexity to basic geometric forms. The process, as well as the resulting appearance, lends itself readily to imitation of other techniques. Among flatweaves of the Caucasus, kilim (slit tapestry) (figs. 8 and 12) lends itself to stepped designs, with right angles forming geometricized edges because of the progression of horizontal lines and short vertical slits; soumak (fig. 9a) lends itself most readily to diagonal patterning in each of four directions, forming acute and obtuse angles, but without intersections at right angles on the horizontal or vertical axes; and cicim (fig. 10a) lends itself most easily to long vertical lines, short horizontal lines, with an approximation of the diagonal line. Similar characterizations may identify Caucasian embroideries, in which stitch placement is determined by the fabric structure. Equilateral cross stitches (fig. 13) or long flat stitches (fig. 1) create structural patterns composed of units of *X*s or long dashes, setting technological limits for patterning.

Embroidery, kilims, cicim, and soumak probably had longer indigenous histories in the Caucasus than did rug weaving. It is likely they exerted a profound influence on the development of designs in local commercial carpet weaving. Both embroideries and early soumaks have a single, narrow border, as do the early historical Caucasian dragon rugs. Multiple borders and distinctive wide main borders may reflect the influence of rug making traditions from regions beyond the Caucasus, probably Persia and Turkey during a period of rapid commercialization of rug weaving in the nineteenth century.[15] In turn, the adaptation of this layout in commercial weaving affected local aesthetic traditions for the weaving of soumak, which at the end of the century also display multiple inner and outer borders and a wide main border.

Conclusion

By the end of the nineteenth century, the Caucasus was an area rich in natural resources (including the renewable resource of wool from flocks) and means of transport, all of which contributed to economic development. The manufacture of knotted pile carpets, often with designs based on embroidery, kilim, cicim, and soumak techniques, became one of the most important commercial activities at that time.

Pile carpets, flatweaves, and embroideries from the Caucasus represent various design traditions, which are interrelated in their use of designs based on technology. Clearly textile arts of the Caucasus reveal an appreciation of graphic design, but more important, in comparison with textile arts of other cultural areas, they exhibit a special appreciation of the integral relationship among design, structure, and technology—the creation of a two-dimensional appearance within the three-dimensional construction inherent in weaving. Further analysis of visual similarities among the textile arts of the Caucasus in relation to structural characteristics may yield a clearer understanding of the historical development of each tradition. The relationship among design, structure, and technology in these textile arts remains a subject worthy of further investigation.

NOTES

1. Sarah B. Sherrill, "Oriental Carpets in Seventeenth- and Eighteenth-century America," *Antiques* (January 1976), 142–167, and C. E. C. Tattersall, *A History of British Carpets* (Essex, 1934). The study of Oriental carpets over the past century has produced a voluminous bibliography. For introductory reading, see May H. Beattie, "On the Making of Carpets," in Donald King and David Sylvester, *The Eastern Carpet in the Western World from the 15th to the 17th Century* [exh. cat., Arts Council of Great Britain] (London, 1983), 106–109; Willem von Bode and Ernst Kühnel, *Antique Rugs from the Near East*, 4th ed., tr. Charles G. Ellis (Ithaca, 1984); Walter Denny, *Oriental Rugs* (New York, 1979); Kurt Erdmann, *Oriental Carpets: An Essay in Their History*, 2nd ed., tr. Charles G. Ellis (New York, 1960); Kurt Erdmann, *Seven Hundred Years of Oriental Carpets*, ed. Hannah Erdmann, tr. May Beattie and H. Herzog (Berkeley and Los Angeles, 1970). For a study of carpets treated as textile arts within the realm of cultural history, see Carol Bier, ed., *Woven from the Soul, Spun from the Heart: Textile Arts of Safavid and Qajar Iran (16th-19th Centuries)* (Washington, 1987).

2. A seminal exhibition organized by the Textile Museum was accompanied by the publication of Anthony N. Landreau and W. Russell Pickering, *From the Bosporus to Samarkand: Flat-Woven Rugs* (Washington, 1969), which has served as a standard reference for many years. Since then, additional publications on flatweaves, as well as tribal and ethnographic materials of the Near East, have made substantial contributions to this field of study: Cathryn Cootner, ed., *Flat-Woven Textiles: The Arthur D. Jenkins Collection* (Washington, 1981); Peter Saunders, *Tribal Visions* (Kentfield, 1980); Yanni Petsopoulos, *Kilims: Flat-woven Tapestry Rugs* (New York, 1979); Belkıs Balpınar Acar, *Kilim-Cicim-Zili-Sumak: Turkish Flatweaves* (Istanbul, 1983); Belkıs Balpınar and Udo Hirsch, *Flatweaves of the Vakiflar Museum Istanbul* (Wesel, 1982); Jenny Housego, *Tribal Rugs: An Introduction to the Weaving of the Tribes of Iran* (London, 1978); Parviz Tanavoli, *Shahsavan: Iranian Rugs and Textiles* (New York, 1985). See also note 12.

3. See Carol Bier, "Weavings from the Caucasus: Tradition and Technology," *Hali* 48 (1989), 17–25 (with annotated bibliography on Caucasian rugs appended). Selected introductory readings on Caucasian rugs include Ian Bennett, *Oriental Rugs* vol. 1, *Caucasian* (London, 1981); Latif Kerimov et al., *Rugs and Carpets from the Caucasus: The Russian Collections* (Leningrad, 1984); Ulrich Schürmann, *Caucasian Rugs* (Braunschweig and London, 1967).

4. See, for example, John Wertime, "The Names, Types, and Functions of Nomadic Weaving in Iran," in Anthony N. Landreau, ed., *Yörük: The Nomadic Weaving Tradition of the Middle East* (Pittsburgh, 1978), 23–26.

5. Şerare Yetkin, *Early Caucasian Carpets in Turkey*, 2 vols. (London, 1978). See also Charles G. Ellis, *Early Caucasian Rugs* (Washington, 1975), and Charles G. Ellis, *Oriental Carpets in the Philadelphia Museum of Art* (Philadelphia, 1988), 132–149.

6. An early suggestion of Ellis 1975, 10–11, further discussed by Michael Franses and Robert Pinner, "Caucasian Carpets in the Victoria and Albert Museum: The Caucasian Collection," *Hali* 3/2 (1980), 96–115.

7. For the purposes of this paper, Irene Emery, *Primary Structures of Fabric* (Washington, 1980), provides the basis for descriptive terminology of structures seen in Caucasian pile carpets and flatweaves.

8. Elisabeth Mikosch, "The Scent of Flowers: Kashmir Shawls in the Collection of The Textile Museum," *Textile Museum Journal* 24 (1985), 6–22; see also Ann P. Rowe, "The Woven Structures of European Shawls in The Textile Museum

Collection," *Textile Museum Journal* 24 (1985), 55–59.

9. Jasleen Dhamija, "Jajim," *Hali* 9/4 (1987), 22–27.

10. Yanni Petsopoulos, "The Qajar Kilims of Sehna," *Hali* 31 (London, 1986), 43–47.

11. John Wertime in Bier 1987, 271.

12. John Wertime, "Flat-Woven Structures Found in Nomadic and Village Weavings from the Near East and Central Asia," *Textile Museum Journal* 18 (1979), 33–55; Wertime, "A Checklist of Flat-Woven Structures Found in Village and Nomadic Weavings from the Near East and Central Asia," *Rug News* ⅔ (September 1980), 2–8; Wertime, "Analyzing and Describing Flat-Woven Structures," *Oriental Carpet and Textile Studies* 1 (1985), 301–304; Wertime, "Weft-Wrapping and Nomadic and Village Flat-Woven Textiles from the Near East and Central Asia," in Cootner 1981, 175–191.

13. Most published diagrams of rug knots are inaccurate. They are usually shown upside down or otherwise tied incorrectly. The only accurate depictions I have come across are those drawn by Milton Sonday in Charles G. Ellis, *Oriental Carpets in the Philadelphia Museum of Art* (Philadelphia, 1988).

14. This carpet is frequently illustrated; perhaps most accessible are the photographs by Cary Wolinsky in Nina Hyde, "Wool—Fabric of History," *National Geographic* 173/5 (May 1988), 552–591.

15. A similar speculative conclusion regarding the large size of late soumaks in relation to the process of commercialization was put forth by Cathryn Cootner in *Hali* 45 (1989), 13.

Contributors

Candace Adelson is an art historian specializing in the decorative arts. She has written numerous articles and collaborated on the organization and catalogues of such international exhibitions as *Le Studiolo d'Isabelle d'Este* (Louvre, Paris, 1975), *Palazzo Vecchio e i Medici* (Palazzo Vecchio, Florence, 1980), *Costumi* (Museo Stibbert, Florence, 1988), and *Circa 1492: Art in the Age of Exploration* (National Gallery of Art, Washington, 1991). In addition, she has contributed to the tapestry and textile section of the National Gallery of Art systematic catalogue and wrote the catalogue of the tapestry collection of the Minneapolis Institute of Arts.

Carol Bier is curator for Eastern Hemisphere collections at the Textile Museum in Washington, where she also chairs the task force on research, publications, library, and education. She received her graduate training at the Oriental Institute of the University of Chicago and at the Institute of Fine Arts, New York University. She has excavated in Turkey, Iran, and Egypt. The organizer of numerous exhibitions on Islamic textiles and Oriental carpets, she has published widely in the fields of Near Eastern art and archaeology.

Guy Delmarcel is professor of art history at the Katholieke Universiteit, Leuven. He was formerly curator of textiles at the Royal Museums of Art and History in Brussels. He has written numerous articles on the history of Flemish tapestry and has published several exhibition catalogues, including *Tapisseries bruxelloises de la pré-Renaissance* (1976), *Tapisseries anciennes d'Enghien* (1980), and *Bruges et la tapisserie* (1987).

Nobuko Kajitani has been a conservator with the department of textile conservation at the Metropolitan Museum of Art since 1966. She began her museum work in 1963 with James W. Rice, Irene Emery, Joseph V. Columbus, Harriet Tidball, and Kate C. Lefferts and developed a special interest in research on the history of fiber and fabric technology, with an emphasis on the long-range preservation of intrinsic qualities of fiber objects. Since 1980 she has been an adjunct professor at the Conservation Center, Institute of Fine Arts, New York University, teaching textile conservation. She has published articles on conservation as well as on the materials and technical features of archaeological fabrics.

Liliane Masschelein-Kleiner is director of the Institut Royal du Patrimoine Artistique, Brussels, where she previously served as head of the department of chemical and physical research. She received a Ph.D. in sciences from the Université Libre de Brussels in 1963, and from 1961 to 1963 she was a fellow of the Belgian

Fonds National de la recherche Scientifique. Her principal interest is in research on natural film-forming substances, ancient and modern dyestuffs, the cleaning of art objects, and the conservation of textiles. She has taught conservation courses in many countries and is an active member of several organizations, including the International Council of Museums, International Institute for Conservation of Historic and Artistic Works, and International Centre for the Study of the Preservation and the Restoration of Cultural Properties.

Lotus Stack is a curator and head of the department of textiles at the Minneapolis Institute of Arts and president of the Textile Society of America. Her exhibition catalogues include *Essential Thread: Tapestry on Wall and Body.*

Edith A. Standen is a consultant to the department of European sculpture and deco-rative arts at the Metropolitan Museum of Art. Before her retirement in 1970, she was an associate curator at the museum in charge of the Textile Study Room. She is the author of *European Post-Medieval Tapestries and Related Hangings in The Metropolitan Museum of Art* (1985) and has published many articles on tapestries and other European textiles.

Isabelle Van Tichelen was formerly research assistant at the Royal Museums of Art and History in Brussels. She received her degree in art history at the Katholieke Universiteit, Leuven, and was a fellow at the Kunsthistorisches Museum in Vienna. She published the exhibition catalogue *Cinq siècles de tapisseries flamandes* (Mechelen, 1989) and is presently collaborating with Guy Delmarcel on the *Dictionary of Marks, Monograms and Signatures on Ancient Flemish Tapestries,* scheduled for publication in 1993.